Hugh Reginald Haweis

Poets in the Pulpit

Hugh Reginald Haweis

Poets in the Pulpit

ISBN/EAN: 9783337777593

Printed in Europe, USA, Canada, Australia, Japan

Cover: Foto ©Thomas Meinert / pixelio.de

More available books at **www.hansebooks.com**

BY THE
REV. H. R. HAWEIS, M.A.
(INCUMBENT OF ST. JAMES, MARYLEBONE)

AUTHOR OF "MUSIC AND MORALS," "THOUGHTS FOR THE TIMES," "SPEECH IN SEASON," "CURRENT COIN," "ARROWS IN THE AIR"

NEW AND CHEAPER EDITION

LONDON
SAMPSON LOW, MARSTON, SEARLE, & RIVINGTON
Limited
St. Dunstan's House
FETTER LANE, FLEET STREET, E.C.
1889

TO

THE RIGHT REV. JAMES FRASER, D.D.,

LORD BISHOP OF MANCHESTER,

THESE DISCOURSES ARE INSCRIBED

WITH FEELINGS OF ADMIRATION AND RESPECT

BY

HUGH REGINALD HAWEIS, M.A.,

INCUMBENT OF ST. JAMES, MARYLEBONE.

PREFACE.

HESE addresses were delivered on a succession of Sundays in the Church of St. James, Marylebone.

They took the place of sermons in a series of services entitled "Sunday Evenings for the People."

They were reported in shorthand, revised by the author, and are now issued in accordance with a very general request.

May the sphere of the Church of England Pulpit be annually enlarged, and may her Preachers learn to press all that is good into the service of God.

H. R. HAWEIS, M.A.

CONTENTS.

		PAGE
I.	LONGFELLOW. SELECTED POEMS	1
II.	TENNYSON. ST. SIMEON STYLITES, AND ST. AGNES	33
III.	TENNYSON. THE VISION OF SIN, AND THE PALACE OF ART	65
IV.	TENNYSON. IN MEMORIAM	87
V.	ROBERT BROWNING. NEW YEAR'S EVE	117
VI.	KEBLE. THE "HIGH CHURCH" AND THE CHRISTIAN YEAR	145
VII.	GEORGE HERBERT. SELECTED POEMS	195
VIII.	WORDSWORTH. DIVERSE POEMS	241
IX.	THE GOLDEN TREASURY. GLEANINGS	261

I.
Longfellow.
SELECTED POEMS.

I.

Longfellow.

SELECTED POEMS.

IT is sometimes thought that an address from the pulpit cannot be good unless it starts with a text. But a right grasp of the Bible should teach us how to find "sermons in stones, and good in everything."

Nothing should be uttered in the pulpit inconsistent with the spirit of Religion, but the Bible need not be incessantly quoted. Let us take a hint from Christ and His Apostles; how did they preach? No doubt they used the Old Testament (the New not being in existence) as something familiar, through which to teach their hearers what was not familiar; it was the schoolmaster leading men to Christ. But the real use of the Old Testament with Christ was, to make men think and feel for themselves; and this indeed is the only kind of teaching worth much in any age. Such teaching is often indirect, but none the less impressive. If you take the Bible only as a textbook, you will be in danger of missing its higher power as a spiritual fountain.

Our Lord's use of texts was peculiar; He usually took them to illustrate the differences between His own teaching and that of the Old Testament, as in the Sermon on the Mount. It was thus He taught: Moses said one thing, I say another. The new was in one sense opposed to the old, yet not destructive of it; it fulfilled and absorbed it. When St. Paul alluded to the Old Testament, it was usually to draw Jews through their favourite oracles to something better; but when he turned from the little Jewish sects to the great outside world, we cease to hear from his lips the Bible texts, instead we have verses from the popular poets and philosophers; as when, on Mars Hill at Athens, he finds an altar to the unknown God, and quotes the poet Aratus (B.C. 270), a native of his own city of Tarsus, in the opening lines of the Phenomena—

Τοῦ γὰρ καὶ γένος ἐσμέν,

"We are also of his offspring;" showing that even the Greek poets had taught that the human race was in some mysterious way bound to the All Father. In the Epistle to Titus, St. Paul alludes to the glaring faults of the Cretan character, lashing the vices of those dissipated islanders with the words of an older poet,—

Κρῆτες ἀεὶ ψεῦσται, κακὰ θηρία, γαστέρες ἀργαί,

which being translated is, "The Cretans were ever liars, evil beasts, lazy gorbels." And if St. Paul did not scruple to point his discourses from popular poets, why should we?

The poets are the men after all—more than statesmen, more than philosophers—who have the deepest hold over, and insight into, the thoughts and feelings of their age. A great student of men once said, "Let who will make the people's laws, let me make the people's songs."

The poet and the prophet in old days meant almost the same thing; the poet was often the true political ruler, as he even now is seldom without direct or indirect political influence. Isaiah was a statesman and popular leader; David, sweet psalmist, was poet and prophet, as well as king. Think of the vast political and social, as well as moral and spiritual influence wielded by Chaucer, Shakespeare, and Milton, down to the present time. And when you study the utterances of contemporary poets, you are really mastering the springs of contemporary life, and, in so far as the poet himself is religious, the central religious thoughts and aspirations of the age. Byron, Wordsworth, Shelley, Tennyson, Longfellow, Browning, Swinbourne, Keble—these are the men who condense the life of your age into words that breathe, and thoughts that burn. They leave among them not a stop untouched, not a chord that is dear and sympathetic unsounded; they cut and polish for us, as one of them has so sweetly sung, those "jewels five words long which on the stretched forefinger of Time sparkle for ever."

Of all living poets (Tennyson not excepted), Longfellow the American has made for himself the widest social popularity. As Dr. Whewell, the famous Master of Trinity College, Cambridge, once said in my hearing, "The sweet and homely melodies of Longfellow have touched a thousand hearts that have been unmoved by the deeper and sometimes abstruse harmonies of Tennyson." But it is Longfellow's fresh, genuine, and tender insight into the religious thoughts and feelings of ordinary human beings, which has made him the minister of hope and the stay of faith in this artificial and doubt-tossed age.

Henry Wadsworth Longfellow is still living. He is seventy-three years (1880) old, being born in 1807, at Portland, Maine, U.S. He was educated at Bowdoin College, where he graduated with honours in 1825. He became Professor of Modern Languages there, and afterwards filled the same post at Harvard College in 1835, and at Cambridge, U.S. in 1836. He has been an extensive traveller throughout Europe, and has translated poems from many different languages, and touched with a master-hand the springs of national life and religion in many lands.

In 1854 he resigned his professorship. In 1868 and 1869 he was with us in England. He went to Oxford, and there they conferred on him the Hon. D.C.L. degree. In 1874 he was nominated for the Lord Rectorship of Glasgow University, and was defeated on a contest, although not by a large majority, by Benjamin Disraeli, Earl of Beaconsfield; and after that he returned to America, and is now living there in his old age, having gone through much suffering, endured many losses, and had a very wide experience of life, and love, and sorrow. Truly he has learned his lesson deeply and well; he has received the good seed into an honest heart, from whence has sprung up for these latter days a good and bountiful harvest. And this thought, that he sowed not for himself alone, but for us—that his work was incomplete without our responsive love and sympathy, seems to have been ever present with him; it has endeared Longfellow to a multitude on either side of the Atlantic; his sympathy reaches across the wide ocean, his voice is heard by those who love it, his teaching felt by those who need it. This power of ministration, this gentle presence of a wise, and genial, and gifted friend—simple, unassuming, yet irresistibly winning—has been beautifully illustrated by him in the lovely Dedication to the " Sea-side and Fireside Poems."

> As one who, walking in the twilight gloom,
>   Hears round about him voices as it darkens;
> And seeing not the forms from which they come,
>   Pauses from time to time, and turns and hearkens;

So, walking here in twilight, oh, my friends,
  I hear your voices, softened by the distance,
And pause, and turn to listen, as each sends
  His words of friendship, comfort, and assistance.

If any thought of mine, or sung or told,
  Has ever given delight or consolation,
Ye have repaid me back a thousand-fold,
  By every friendly sign or salutation.

Thanks for the sympathies that ye have shown!
  Thanks for each kindly word, each silent token,
That teaches me, when seeming most alone,
  Friends are around us, though no word be spoken;—

Kind messages, that pass from land to land;
  Kind letters, that betray the heart's deep history,
In which we feel the pressure of a hand,
  One touch of fire, and all the rest is mystery!—

The pleasant books, that silently among
  Our household treasures take familiar places,
And are to us as if a living tongue
  Spake from the printed leaves or pictured faces.

Perhaps on earth I never shall behold,
  With eye of sense, your outward form and semblance;
Therefore to me ye never will grow old,
  But live for ever young in my remembrance.

Never grow old, nor change, nor pass away!
  Your gentle voices will flow on for ever,—
When life grows bare, and tarnished with decay,
  As through a lifeless landscape flows a river.

Not chance of birth or place has made us friends,
    Being oftentimes of different tongues and nations;
But the endeavour for the self-same ends,
    With the same hopes, and fears, and aspirations.

Therefore I hope to join your sea-side walk,
    Saddened, and mostly silent, with emotion;
Not interrupting with intrusive talk
    The grand, majestic symphonies of ocean.

Therefore I hope, as no unwelcome guest,
    At your warm fireside, when the lamps are lighted,
To have my place reserved among the rest,
    Nor stand as one unsought and uninvited!

Now to-night, let me try and gather up, as in a brief though illustrated summary, some of the noblest qualities of this poet's teaching, as I dwell upon (I.) Longfellow's Natural Religion, (II.) Longfellow's View of Death, (III.) Longfellow's Endeavour after the Higher Life, (IV.) Longfellow's Philanthropy and Charity, (V.) Longfellow's Faith and Hope.

I. LONGFELLOW'S NATURAL RELIGION.—There are immense gains in culture and civilization, but we lose some things; we lose the sharp keen primitive taste—" the great glad, aboriginal instincts," as Emerson calls them—the healthy loves and hates—aye, and the healthy response of the soul to God. We miss the natural influences which the sweet things of nature are designed to bring home to our hearts.

We go with blunted perceptions and bleared eyes to God's beautiful world; we fail to hear the secrets of the harmonious seasons, we sit down with jaded appetites to the banquet of the blooming earth, and the light of heaven is dim.

But what constitutes the religious heart is just this—to be able to lift up our eyes and see, as Henry Melville puts it, the whole world " burning with Deity ! "

And what constitutes the eye of the poet is this, that he sees what others cannot see. What made Turner a great painter was, that he could catch those effects of light and shade, of evanescent colour, and register them so as to make others see them and love them too. " I never saw such effects in nature," said a buyer to Turner. " No," replied the master; "but don't you wish you could?"

It requires a special cultivated faculty before you can see what the poets and artists can see in outward nature. And it requires the tender heart and fresh susceptibilities before you can read the great lessons of natural religion in the outward and visible universe, and look up through nature to nature's God.

It is because this faculty is so fresh, this habit so confirmed in Longfellow, that I commend him specially to this busy, hurrying, striving age, over which his sweet temper has gained such a happy control. Longfellow, in the happy solitudes of Nature, cannot choose but feel and see God; he listens to the voices of the Woodlands, and the Ocean, and the Night, as well as to those of the Temple and the Fire-side.

Hear him, or rather over-hear him, in the summer woods,—

> Into the blithe and breathing air,
>   Into the solemn wood—
> Solemn and silent everywhere,
> Nature with folded hands seemed there—
>   Like one in prayer I stood.

And wherever he turns divine whispers reach his unspoiled heart, and his words flow forth with the gentle grace and simplicity of a child's prayer:

> Wondrous truths, and manifold as wondrous,
>   God has written in those stars above;

But not less in the bright flow'rets under us,
   Stands the revelation of His love.

Bright and glorious is that revelation,
   Written all over this great world of ours,
Making evident our own creation—
   In these stars of earth, these golden flowers.

And the poet, faithful and far-seeing,
   Sees, alike in stars and flowers, a part
Of the self-same universal being
   Which is throbbing in his brain and heart.

Does it not almost seem to lead up to the climax of that more concisely inspired utterance of the Apostle Paul, when he too is bidding men look through creation to the Creator: "Because that which may be known of God is manifest in us, for God hath showed it unto us. For the invisible things of Him from the creation of the world are clearly seen, being understood by the things that are made, even His eternal power and Godhead." Romans ii. 20.

II. LONGFELLOW ON DEATH.—If there is one thing which paralyzes and depresses us in the midst of contemplating beautiful things in the outward world, it is the depressing effect of the spectacle of Death, with its inseparable pain and suffering. Who shall lighten for us the burden of death? Who shall take from the grave its darkness, and from death its bitterness? Many a brave and bright spirit has gone on its way rejoicing, until it came upon the veiled figure and the yawning abyss. It is especially on all these sad and grim subjects that Longfellow is sweetly and nobly inspired. The pain of separation—the terror of dissolution, vanishes beneath his ardent touch; and those who are naturally paralyzed and prostrated by the spectacle of humanity passing into apparent darkness and oblivion, are suddenly lifted up and comforted. Even that most dismal of all symbols and reminders of mortality, a close city churchyard, is suffused beneath his gaze with delicate and poetic emotion. You may have noticed some of our own city grave-yards. Many of them, it is true, have now been turned into bright places for springing flowers; but others remain, do what you will to them, dismal, and dreary, and lonely; and when we pass, the sight of these mouldering stones behind the iron railings, and the green rank grass, makes our hearts sink within us, as we think of the decaying bodies which lie beneath. Yet even these seem to acquire new pathos, and derive a certain glory, from the brightness of the poet's spirit, and his first thought is one of deep rest:—

All was ended now, and the hope, and the fear, and the sorrow—
All the aching of heart, the restless unsatisfied longing,—
All the dull deep pain, and constant anguish of patience!
* * * * * * *
In the heart of the city they lie, unknown and unnoticed.
Daily the tides of life go ebbing and flowing beside them;
Thousands of throbbing hearts, where theirs are at rest for ever;
Thousands of aching brains, where theirs no longer are busy;
Thousands of toiling hands, where theirs have ceased from their labours;
Thousands of weary feet, where theirs have completed their journey!

And whether he touches on the passing away of a little child in the first dawn of life, or a young man or woman taken in the glowing bloom of youth, or the more mature companion of our later years, there is the same undefinable glow of hope and aspiration, and the same recurrent feeling that they are not dead, but gone before—the very message which every one who has lost a dear friend longs to receive. Ah! we often hear it from lips which pronounce it apparently without feeling it, and are not able to convey to those who want to feel it, the precious faith in the existence, perchance the presence, of the dear, the forever-remembered dead! Then are the words of the true and faithful poet helpful. He never sounds the note of despair; doubt never sweeps darkly across his soul. But the spirit world itself becomes visible to him; he is looking out from the loneliness of his life with the eyes of an inspired seer, and we sit and listen at his feet whilst he pours forth, without constraint or effort, such a flood of spiritual emotion that our drooping souls are indeed lifted up with the hope that is full of immortality. Hear him on the death of little children :—

> There is a Reaper, whose name is Death,
>   And, with his sickle keen,
> He reaps the bearded grain at a breath,
>   And the flowers that grow between.
>
> "Shall I have nought that is fair?" saith he;
>   "Have nought but the bearded grain?
> "Though the breath of these flowers is sweet to me,
>   "I will give them all back again."
>
> He gazed at the flowers with tearful eyes,
>   He kissed their drooping leaves.
> It was for the Lord of Paradise
>   He bound them in his sheaves.

"My Lord has need of these flow'rets gay,"
   The Reaper said, and smiled;
"Dear tokens of the earth are they,
   Where He was once a child.

"They shall all bloom in fields of light,
   Transplanted by my care;
And saints upon their garments white
   These sacred blossoms wear."

And the mother gave, in tears and pain,
   The flowers she most did love;
She knew she should find them all again
   In the fields of light above.

Oh, not in cruelty, not in wrath,
   The Reaper came that day;
'Twas an angel visited the green earth,
   And took the flowers away.

And equally sweet and searching is the note of resignation sounded on the passing away of those who are young and beautiful in the bloom of years:—

There is no flock, however watched and tended,
   But one dead lamb is there!
There is no fireside, howsoe'er defended,
   But has one vacant chair!

The air is full of farewells to the dying,
   And mournings for the dead;
The heart of Rachel, for her children crying,
   Will not be comforted!

Let us be patient ! These severe afflictions
   Not from the ground arise ;
But oftentimes celestial benedictions
   Assume this dark disguise.

*   *   *   *   *   *

There is no death ! What seems so is transition ;
   This life of mortal breath
Is but a suburb of the life elysian,
   Whose portal we call Death.

She is not dead, the child of our affection,
   But gone unto that school
Where she no longer needs our poor protection,
   And Christ himself doth rule.

In that great cloister's stillness and seclusion,
   By guardian angels led,
Safe from temptation, safe from sin's pollution,
   She lives, whom we call dead.

*   *   *   *   *   *

Not as a child shall we again behold her ;
   For when, with raptures wild,
In our embraces we again enfold her,
   She will not be a child ;

But a fair maiden, in her Father's mansion,
   Clothed with celestial grace ;
And beautiful with all the soul's expansion,
   Shall we behold her face.

And though at times, impetuous with emotion,
   And anguish long suppressed,

> The swelling heart heaves, moaning like the ocean
>   That cannot be at rest;
>
> We will be patient, and assuage the feeling
>   We may not wholly stay;
> By silence sanctifying, not concealing,
>   The grief that must have way.

Or again, when he deals with the more mature, and far more irreparable losses:

> They, the holy ones and weakly,
>   Who the cross of suffering bore,
> Folded their pale hands so meekly,
>   Spake with us on earth no more!
>
> And with them the Being Beauteous,
>   Who unto my youth was given,
> More than all things else to love me,
>   And is now a saint in heaven.
>
> With a slow and noiseless footstep
>   Comes that messenger divine,
> Takes the vacant chair beside me,
>   Lays her gentle hand in mine.
>
> And she sits and gazes at me
>   With those deep and tender eyes,—
> Like the stars, so still and saint-like,
>   Looking downward from the skies.
>
> Utter'd not, yet comprehended,
>   Is the spirit's noiseless prayer,—
> Soft rebukes, in blessings ended,
>   Breathing from her lips of air.

> Oh, though oft depressed and lonely,
>   All my fears are laid aside,
> If I but remember only
>   Such as these have lived and died.

Is not death changed? is not the weight lifted? is not One felt to be very near us, bearing our sorrow, and carrying our griefs?

> O holy trust! O endless sense of rest!
>   Like the beloved John,
> To lay his head upon the Saviour's breast,
>   And thus to journey on!

This grasp of things unseen—this sense of the ever present surroundings of the world of spirits—this abiding trust in the love which has passed beyond the grave, and gate of death, does it not seem to be yet another spiritual echo of the great Apostle's words—"O death, where is thy sting? O grave, where is thy victory?"

III. LONGFELLOW'S ENDEAVOUR AFTER THE HIGHER LIFE.—But perhaps, after all, what has gained the firmest hold over the English mind are, not the meditations on death, but the practical grappling with the affairs of every-day life, the trumpet calls to duty, the oft declared need for patience, perseverance, and tireless endeavour.

There is a practical sense about Longfellow which redeems him from every charge of sentimentality. If you ever find him indulging in anything like what we may call "sentiment," it is only to nerve and inspire us with energy for manly action; and I should be unjust to the genius of the greatest American poet if I did not here remind you of his oft repeated "Psalm of Life."

> Tell me not, in mournful numbers,
>   Life is but an empty dream !
> For the soul is dead that slumbers,
>   And things are not what they seem.
>
> Life is real ! Life is earnest !
>   And the grave is not its goal :
> " Dust thou art, to dust returnest,"
>   Was not spoken of the soul.
>
> Not enjoyment, and not sorrow,
>   Is our destined end or way ;
> But to act that each to-morrow
>   Finds us farther than to-day.
>
> Art is long, and time is fleeting,
>   And our hearts, though stout and brave,
> Still, like muffled drums, are beating
>   Funeral marches to the grave.
>
> In the world's broad field of battle,
>   In the bivouac life,

> Be not like dumb, driven cattle!
>   Be a hero in the strife!
>
> Trust no Future, howe'er pleasant!
>   Let the dead Past bury its dead!
> Act,—act in the living Present!
>   Heart within, and God o'erhead!
>
> Lives of great men all remind us
>   We can make our lives sublime,
> And departing, leave behind us
>   Footprints on the sands of time :
>
> Footprints, that perhaps another,
>   Sailing o'er life's solemn main,
> A forlorn and shipwrecked brother,
>   Seeing, shall take heart again.
>
> Let us, then, be up and doing,
>   With a heart for any fate;
> Still achieving, still pursuing,
>   Learn to labour and to wait.

And in the matter of earnest moral activity there is another poem, called the "Ladder of St. Augustine," much less known, but also sounding a practical note, the opening lines of which are interesting because they remind us of Tennyson's lines referring to the same quotation from St. Augustine.

> I hold it truth, with him who sings
>   To one clear harp in divers tones,

That men may rise on stepping-stones
   Of their dead selves to higher things.

Many persons on reading the " In Memoriam,"
have inquired who it is that is referred to. Longfellow informs us :—

Saint Augustine ! well hast thou said
   That of our vices we can frame
A ladder, if we will but tread
   Beneath our feet each deed of shame !

All common things—each day's events
   That with the hour begin and end,
Our pleasures and our discontents,
   Are rounds by which we may ascend.

The low desire—the base design
   That makes another's virtues less,
The revel of the giddy wine,
   And all occasions of excess ;

The longing for ignoble things,
   The strife for triumph more than truth,
The hardening of the heart, that brings
   Irreverence for the dreams of youth ;

All thoughts of ill—all evil deeds
   That have their root in thoughts of ill,
Whatever hinders or impedes
   The action of the nobler will,—

All these must first be trampled down
   Beneath our feet, if we would gain,

> In the bright field of Fair Renown,
>   The right of eminent domain!

*   *   *   *   *   *

> The heights by great men reached and kept,
>   Were not attained by sudden flight;
> But they, while their companions slept,
>   Were toiling upward in the night.
>
> Standing on what too long we bore,
>   With shoulders bent and downcast eyes,
> We may discern, unseen before,
>   A path to higher destinies.
>
> Nor deem the irrevocable past
>   As wholly wasted, wholly vain,
> If, rising on its wrecks, at last
>   To something nobler we attain.

So there is practical, wise, and solid counsel for us here, although perhaps in the "Psalm of Life" Longfellow is sweetest and most powerful—as, indeed, there he is most admirably concise.

IV. LONGFELLOW'S PHILANTHROPY AND CHARITY.—Yet the strictly philanthropic and charitable side of the poet remains; and when he calls us to remember the sufferings he has so deeply felt himself, and bids us turn away from our own hours of selfishness or idle enjoyment, there seems to be a lesson for us, especially in the present day, which is full of so much selfishness, pleasure seeking, money making, and money spending, without a care by those who have for those who want, so that if a man struggles a little to the front himself, he heeds not what becomes of his brother who toils—when, if you have enough for yourselves you cease to feel for the sufferings of others—and, surrounded by comforts, you care not who " goes bare, goes bare."

Friends, whilst at this bitter Christmas season* your houses are lighted up with feasting, and revelry and the songs of rejoicing are ringing through your rooms—a cry of distress comes up, which you cannot well drown, and which you should never forget.

You cannot take up a newspaper without reading of fearful distress in the north of England, where trade is paralyzed to such an extent that hundreds and thousands cannot get the necessaries of life. It is not only the ordinary workman, but the small trader, and the small dealer with whom he deals—the retail dealer—seem at last

---

* The winter of 1878 was one of unusual severity, coincident with exceptional commercial depression.

to be suffering. And this sad cry, which has begun too early in the winter, is likely to go on increasing until the spring. And although the present distress may be exceptional—remember, the poor ye have always with you—there is never a dearth of famine, or pain, or poverty; and you have no right to be comfortable in your warm homes, unless you have done what you can for the homeless—or to sit at your Christmas feasts, unless you have tried to feed the hungry—or to rejoice, unless you have helped to comfort the afflicted.

The poet shall here take his place in the pulpit, and preach you this short but powerful sermon :—

> I have a vague remembrance
>   Of a story that is told,
> In some ancient Spanish legend,
>   Or chronicle of old.
>
> It was when brave King Sanchez,
>   Was before Zamora slain,
> And his great besieging army
>   Lay encamped upon the plain.
>
> Don Diego de Ordoñez
>   Sallied forth in front of all,
> And shouted loud his challenge
>   To the warders on the wall.

All the people of Zamora,
  Both born and the unborn,
As traitors did he challenge,
  With taunting words of scorn:

The living, in their houses;
  And in their graves, the dead;
And the waters of their rivers,
  And their wine, and oil, and bread!

There is a greater army,
  That besets us round with strife,—
A starving, numberless army,
  At all the gates of life.

The poverty-stricken millions,
  Who challenge our wine and bread,
And impeach us all as traitors,
  Both the living and the dead.

And whenever I sit at the banquet,
  Where the feast and song are high,
Amid the mirth and the music
  I can hear that fearful cry.

And hollow and haggard faces
  Look into the lighted hall,
And wasted hands are extended
  To catch the crumbs that fall.

For within there is light and plenty,
  And odours fill the air;
But without there is cold and darkness,
  And hunger and despair.

> And there in the camp of famine,
> In wind, and cold, and rain,
> Christ, the great Lord of the army,
> Lies dead upon the plain!

V. LONGFELLOW'S FAITH AND HOPE.—So with thoughts like these we come to our last poem of "The Christmas Bells." They are about to sound a very sad peal to some of us, with much of mournful irony, when we think how far we are from that peace on earth and good will towards men of which they are meant to remind us. And some perhaps are inclined to take a pessimist view of life, as they recall the bright and beneficent doctrines of Christianity, and perceive how little effect they have in allaying, not only the distress and sorrow, but the violence and malice of the world about us. And others ask, where is God? Why does He not show His arm? Why does He not disperse want, and hunger, and sin? Why does He not put a stop to war? If people are Christians, and the kingdoms of this world are becoming the kingdoms of our God and of His Christ, why does not Christianity triumph? why do not men settle disputes by arbitration? why do nations rise one against another? why are the resources of industry and science lavished on fearful and diabolical engines, to enable men to murder those who never did them any harm, and against whom they have no unfriendly feeling, but who are hurled against each other in masses, both armies perhaps professing the same Christianity—as was the case in the great war between North and South America, or between France and Prussia, or between England, Italy, France, and Russia, in the Crimea—Christian people, belonging maybe to different churches, but still Christian people? And why are thousands of homes made miserable, by loss, and want, and despair, whilst Christmas bells are ringing out "Peace on earth and good will towards men"? Ah! you have sometimes felt inclined to despair of humanity. But despair is not the note of the spiritual life; the victory lies not with the seen and temporal, but with the things unseen and eternal; and you are pessimists in spite of yourselves. You who have ceased to believe in the progress of right and the victory of good, may be recalled to a healthier and nobler view by the indomitable hopefulness and deep trust to be found in the utterances of Longfellow, and, I significantly add, Tennyson. So the two great characteristic poets of the Old and New Worlds, amid our infidelities, our pessimist views of life, our failures, and our sins, still hold high the torch of redemptive good—still bear aloft the soiled and tattered banner of our heavenly King—still proclaim that all is well, as those that hear the " deeper voice beyond the storm." And so I am not ashamed to sound the same note at this festival of Christmas, and to keep before a world darkened with malice and stained with bloodshed the immortal refrain of the Christmas Bells.

> I heard the bells on Christmas-day
> Their old familiar carols play,
>   And wild and sweet
>   The words repeat
> Of peace on earth, good will to men!
>
> And thought how, as the day had come,
> The belfries of all Christendom
>   Had rolled along
>   The unbroken song
> Of peace on earth, good will to men!
>
> Till, ringing, singing on its way,
> The world revolved from night to-day,
>   A voice, a chime,
>   A chant sublime,
> Of peace on earth, good will to men!

Then from each black, accursed mouth
The canon thundered, in the South,
  And with the sound
  The carols drowned
Of peace on earth, good will to men!

It was as if an earthquake rent
The hearthstones of a continent,
  And made forlorn
  The households born
Of peace on earth, good will to men!

And in despair I bowed my head:
"There is no peace on earth," I said;
  "For hate is strong,
  And mocks the song
Of peace on earth, good will to men!"

Then pealed the bells more loud and deep:
"God is not dead, nor doth He sleep!
  The wrong shall fail,
  The right prevail,
With peace on earth, good will to men!

This is the *Resurgam* of hope; I leave it with you to-night. In it Longfellow conducts us to the very threshold of the New Year, with the vigour of inexhaustible life.

Take home to your hearts the warmth of his sweet natural religion; take home the peaceful and quiet contemplation of death and the grave, and the bright glimpses of the shining fields beyond;

take home his manly courage, his earnest endeavour after all that is noble, and sweet, and upward; take home his unstained aspirations, his sense and belief in the triumph of good. He sends you forth into the New Year, but he bids you tread its threshold with a firm and light step; before you lies an unknown, untravelled world.

> Into what land of harvests, what plantations,
> Bright with Autumnal foliage and the glow
>   Of sunsets burning low;
> Beneath what midnight skies, whose constellations
> Light up the spacious avenues between
>   This world and the unseen;—
>
> Amid what friendly greetings and caresses,
> What households, though not alien, yet not mine,
>   What bowers of rest divine;
> To what temptations in lone wildernesses,
> What famine of the heart, what pain and loss,
>   The bearing of what cross,—
>
> I do not know; nor will I vainly question
> Those pages of the mystic book which hold
>   The story still untold;
> But without rash conjecture or suggestion,
> Turn its last leaves, in reverence and good heed,
>   Until " The End " I read.

II.

Tennyson.

ST. SIMEON STYLITES AND ST. AGNES.

D

II.

Tennyson.

ST. SIMEON STYLITES AND ST. AGNES.

 SPECIAL introduction to Tennyson might be desirable, but I can only, in the time and space at my disposal, attempt to place him generally before you, and point to some of the influences which formed him, and upon which he has reacted.

Tennyson is emphatically the man of his age; he is intimately connected, in their wider aspects, with the political, social, and intellectual, as well as the poetical and spiritual, movements of the nineteenth century.

Born in 1809, he came into public notice between 1830-40, and soon embodied in poetic literature the romantic movement then at its zenith on the continent. But the literary and artistic movement, at home and abroad was only a part of a general upheaval, in politics and religion.

In 1830 the revolution broke out in Paris, and was followed in England by a long and successful agitation for Reform. Whilst in literature the forces set loose by the severe continental agitation took splendid and spontaneous shape in the wide embracing and inexhaustible excursions of Scott into untrodden realms of poetry, history, and romance; Coleridge gave expression to the mystic side of an intense and earnest religious philosophy; Southey added clearness and common sense to every subject he touched; Byron uttered the fierce revolt of his age against social fetters, hypocrisy, and shams—not always wisely, but too well; Shelley seized the finer elements of the deep spiritual reaction against dogmatic theology, and bade the world bathe once more in the Arethusan fountain of wild unsullied nature; Wordsworth, mellow with years and wisdom, standing a little apart from the strife of tongues, was yet deeply affected by the new social and political ideas, but sought the calm they could not give in quiet contemplation; and with an eye turned now upon the fair sky, and sea, and earth, and now inwardly upon the panorama of the soul, uttered thoughts so high, and sweet, and gentle, that his own age could hardly hear them aright, until the lips of stormier bards had grown silent.

Tennyson was Wordsworth's successor in the Laureateship. He received that poet wreath, as he himself says, " greener from the brows of him (Wordsworth) that uttered nothing base;" and he himself has nobly followed in that shining track.

Before I proceed to mark the characteristic qualities of Tennyson—before I dwell on his depth and power of thought, his keen and wide range of sympathy, or point out the great spirituality and religiousness of his mind, I note in him the primal qualities common to all true poets. Let us define Poetry. "Poetry," says John Stuart Mill, "is the expression of thought coloured by emotion or feeling, expressed in metrical language, and overheard." When first I read the definition I thought it cumbersome and too long; but the more I pondered it, the more complete and adequate did it appear to be. Read it through once more: " Poetry is thought coloured by emotion or feeling, expressed in metrical language, and overheard." Notice the significance of "overheard." The poet is not like an orator, he does not appeal directly to his audience; he is not a mere rhetorician—otherwise poetry might be merely thought coloured by emotion or feeling. That is oratory. It is combined, after a manner in art, often with a certain rhythmic flow and cadence, though without metre. And all high and impassioned, or even angry utterance, runs naturally into a sort of rhythm, which is not necessarily poetry; oratory may be poetical, without being poetry. But the poet, though he does not address you directly, allows you to listen to what he has to say; standing apart, he still takes you sympathetically into his confidence, therefore he is by you "*overheard.*"

I. ACTIVE AND PASSIVE SENSIBILITY.—Now to proceed; what is the first indispensable quality for a poet? It is sensibility; that exquisite response to the external world, coupled with a certain intense perception of the interior life. Poetic sensibility is both active and passive. When the poet's mind is intensely and actively possessed, he is able to impress all things with his mood—he imposes his own emotional atmosphere on his surroundings.

"He sees himself in all he sees."

That is the active part of sensibility.

Then there is the passive side. The poet stands with open heart and mind, ready to receive and register impressions. He is the great High Priest of nature. He is here to interpret her mandates, to overhear her secret whispers long before he himself is overheard of men. His heart beats in time with the universe; he is one with all nature in praise, and in sympathy with all human beings in sorrow and joy. His mind is like that sensitive plate, which, steeped in chemicals, retains every gradation of light and shade; nay, more than this, for the poet reflects the changing hues of emotion as well, and chronicles its vigour and varying temperatures; he is like the Æolian lyre, responsive and melodious to the faintest breath of wind. He falls into a trance, having his eyes open, and sees the kingdoms of heaven and earth, and the glory of them.

There are many illustrious examples of pure writers among us at the present time possessing this high active and passive sensitiveness. They are poetic although they do not write poetry. John Ruskin is a great poet, and some of the finest of modern poetical utterances are to be found in his writings. I know nothing more magnificent, for instance, than the description of the *Old Fighting Temeraire* being towed to her last resting-place—a description in which the external object first impresses the passive mind, and the mind in its turn is roused into an atmospheric excitement, which at last completely reacts upon, and impresses with its own stamp, the pathetic symbol of French defeat and English victory.

Tennyson has in a high degree this active poetic sensibility, this power of impressing his mood upon outward nature. Hear the lone Œnone as she watches her beloved pine forests on the dewy slopes of Ida. The scene is saddened with her own sad soul; every object is coloured by the grief and passion of her irreparable loss, as she marks the tall pines—

> " From beneath
> Whose thick mysterious boughs, in the dark morn,
> The panther's roar came muffled, while I sat
> Low in the valley. Never, never more
> Shall lone Œnone see the morning mist
> Sweep through them ; never see them overlaid

> With narrow moon-lit slips of silver cloud,
> Between the loud stream and the trembling stars."

It is to her over-excited nervous system that the music of the leaping cataract roars so hoarsely —a loud stream; it is through her tears that, as she looks up, the pitiless cold fires become "trembling stars;" it is the self-impressing power of excited sensibility. The poets teem with examples. How has night been variously coloured by their imperious moods! In the happy spirit of Longfellow's verse, "The night shall be filled with music." But to one suffering from an immense loss—

> "All night the darkness seemed to flow
> Beside me, in my utter woe."

Or to one smarting under a self-inflicted heart wound, inflicted in youth—

> "Drug thy memories lest thou learn it,
> Lest thy heart be put to proof,
> In the dead unhappy night, and when the rain is on the roof."

II. THE POWER OF EXPRESSION.— The second poetic quality is the power of expression; the poet invents those golden sentences which in a few words sum a volume of thought, a lifetime of feeling.

His thought takes form in admirably selected periods, which exactly reproduce, without periphrasis or explanation, the thought or impulse that stirs him; and often an exquisite image or subtly chosen adjective comes to his aid, than which nothing fitter can be imagined. How lovely are the fast-fixed things of childish memory, that outlast the shocks of time and all the troubled days of middle life!

> "Those priceless flowers, which in the rudest wind
> Never grow sere, when rooted in the garden of the mind."

How noble and dignified are the deliverances of memory to one who recalls, not only in his own life, but in the life of the world, the scenes and events of the past, until like strains of weird melody come back to us the voices of the dead, the legend of the ages,

> "And thou listenest the lordly music
> Flowing from the illimitable years!"

III. WORD-PAINTING.—The third indispensable quality is word-painting, or the power of producing to the mind's eye a whole picture, with a few touches. The goddesses in the vale of Ida—

> "And at their feet the crocus brake like fire."

No colour art could raise a more dazzling glimpse. Or here, in a river winding to its source amongst the distant hills, we have a study in words, which reminds us of a David Cox, or a Copley Fielding, as the poet stands

> "To watch the long bright river, drawing slowly
> His waters from the purple hills."

Or here is a vignette of bells :—

> "As one who from a casement leans his head
> When midnight bells cease ringing suddenly,
> And the old year is dead!"

Or here is a study in white and sepia, or grey and silver :—

> "A still salt pool, locked in with bars of sand,
> Upon the shore, that hears all night
> The plunging seas draw backward from the land
> Their moon-lit waters white."

IV.—No true poet is without a fourth, and allied quality, which Richard Hutton has called the physical atmosphere of words. It is the semi-musical use of words, exciting an emotion, almost independently of their sense or logical construction—a something which gives a feeling of the place through the sound; as when Sir Bedivere, loth to hurl the good sword Excalibur into the mere, returns to the dying King Arthur, and makes answer,—

> "I heard the ripple washing in the reeds,
> And the wild water lapping on the crag,"

we are at once on the brink of the broad lake in the moonlight. Or in that ambrosial passage,—

> "O, art thou sighing for Lebanon,
> Dark cedar, in the long breeze which streams
> From thy delicious East?"

"Sighing for Lebanon!" the very feeling of Eden comes upon us. Or who cannot feel the sea coast and the sea at night in olden time in

> "Only the rounded moon
> Through the tall oriel on the rolling sea"?

Or some long avenue of odorous limes, like the Trinity Avenue at the Cambridge "backs" in spring, in

> "The moan of doves in immemorial elms,
> And murmuring of innumerable bees."

This power of swaying words to the rhythm of poetic sensibility is one of Tennyson's finest enchantments. Thus, sensibility active and passive, expression, word-painting, and the physical atmosphere of words, combined with artistic finish, are the primal qualities indispensable to all poets; and Tennyson has them in the highest degree.

V. TENNYSON'S CHARACTERISTICS. — But others have had the word-power, the sensibility, the artistic finish. I pass to notice that exceptional combination which constitutes Tennyson's special strength. If I were asked what are Tennyson's chief characteristics, I should reply,

1st. His depth and sobriety of thought.
2nd. His wide sympathies.
3rd. His moral and religious instincts.

First characteristic—Depth and Sobriety of Thought. We have had brilliant poets unable to think, and powerful thinkers unable to express their thoughts and feelings poetically; we have had passionate thinkers fully endowed with expression, but wanting in judgment, proportion, and sobriety. Tennyson is distinguished by depth of thought and sobriety of judgment. How dignified is his address to Queen Victoria, on receiving from her the Laureate's crown! What a contrast to the sort of poor adulation, often lavished upon the reigning sovereign! how full of just perception, how delicately true!

"Her court was pure, her life serene;
  God gave her peace, her land reposed.
  A thousand claims to reverence closed,
In her as Mother, Wife, and Queen.

And statesmen at her council met,
  Who knew the seasons when to take
  Occasion by the hand, and make
The bounds of freedom wider yet,

By shaping some august decree,
  Which kept her throne unshaken still,
  Broad-based upon her people's will,
And compassed by th' inviolate sea."

Or when, at a very critical time in our country's history, he touches on freedom—instead of flaming out into anything like revolution, he uses language which, after the lapse of years, although written at a moment of great public excitement, can still be read with approval—he seizes the heart of political freedom, which is universally sound, and treats it apart from its accidental surroundings. The prophet or poet sees in everything the untransitory element, the residuum of human and universal interest, therefore he writes what is true for the ages, " speaks to time and eternity."

"You ask me why, though ill at ease,
  Within this region I subsist,

Whose spirits falter in the mist,
And languish for the purple seas?

It is the land that freemen till,
  That sober-suited Freedom chose—
  The land where, girt with friends or foes,
A man may speak the thing he will.

A land of settled government,
  A land of just and old renown,
  Where freedom broadens slowly down
From precedent to precedent.

Where faction seldom gathers head;
  But, by degrees to fulness wrought,
  The strength of some diffusive thought
Hath time and space to work and spread."

Hear him now on the critical subject of war, a topic which seems to rouse the hot blood of Englishmen whenever it is mentioned in connexion with impending or actual struggle. How sober and impressive are his views!

" If New and Old disastrous feud
Must ever shock, like armèd foes,—
And this be true till time shall close,
That principles are rained in blood,—

Not yet the wise of heart would cease
To hold his hope through shame and guilt;
But, with his hand against the hilt,
Would pace the troubled land, like Peace.

> Not less though dogs of faction bay,
> Would serve his kind in deed and word,—
> Certain if knowledge bring the sword,
> That knowledge takes the sword away;
>
> Would love the gleams of good that broke
> From either side, nor veil his eyes;
> And if some dreadful need should rise,
> Would strike, and firmly, and one stroke."

Here everything is reasoned, sober, balanced. But he more delights to pass on to the prophetic vision, in which he sees war disappearing finally. Our poet, like all good men and all good women, is at the bottom an optimist. He won't believe we are always going to be struggling and fighting; he believes in the reign of peace, and goes on working and hoping for the cause, through evil report and good report; so that his vision endured—

> "Till the war-drum throbb'd no longer, and the battle flags were furl'd,
> In the parliament of man, the federation of the world.
> There the common sense of most shall hold a fretful realm in awe,
> And the kindly earth shall slumber, lapt in universal law."

Nor is he less wise and hopeful when facing the great social questions of the time, which he calls the " fair new forms that float about the threshold of an age." How sound and sweet are his words on that great question of the redistribution of property. Some people seem to get all, and others nothing. How much envy is there of the great hereditary landowners, who are buying up everything, and treating people as serfs, or ejecting them at will, clearing a wide country, as we have cleared Scotland, in order to make it a happy hunting-ground for the rich — natural rights ignored, and a state of things created which is now making it difficult for small farmers to live. In view of which Tennyson looks forward to a time when,

> "Wealth will no more rest on mounded heaps,
> But, smit with freer light, shall slowly melt,
> In many streams, to fatten lower lands,
> And light shall spread, and man be liker man,
> Through all the seasons of the golden year."

I note one more phase of his sobriety of feeling; it is where he touches on sorrow. I am specially glad, when speaking of Tennyson's moderation, to point out to you the delicate manner in which he handles sorrow and grief in another's case, just as we shall see by-and-by how forcibly he handles his own sorrow and grief; for Tennyson has been accused of sentimentality, and of whining and weeping in a sort of maudlin way, instead of bearing his troubles like a man; and of not really comforting other people, because he himself is apt to fall into such a weak mood when he contemplates their sorrows or his own. To this oft-repeated charge, which has been chiefly brought against the "In Memoriam" as destructive of its wholesome tendency, the lines "to J. S." (John Sterling, I believe, the friend of Carlyle) are a fit reply. They contain all that a sympathizing friend could say, without intruding too far into the sorrow of others or losing heart in one's own :—

> "'Tis strange that those we lean on most,
>   Those in whose laps our limbs are nursed,
> Fall into shadow, soonest lost:
>   Those we love first are taken first.
>
> God gives us love. Something to love
>   He lends us; but, when love is grown
> To ripeness, that on which it throve
>   Falls off, and love is left alone.
>   *   *   *   *
> I knew your brother; his mute dust
>   I honour, and his living worth :
> A man more pure, and bold, and just,
>   Was never born into the earth.

I have not looked upon you nigh
  Since that dear soul hath fall'n asleep.
Great Nature is more wise than I,
  I will not tell you not to weep.

* * * * *

Let grief be her own mistress still;
  She loveth her own anguish deep,
More than much pleasure. Let her will
  Be done—to weep or not to weep.

I will not say, ' God's ordinance
  Of death is blown in every wind;"
For that is not a common chance,
  That takes away a noble mind.

His memory long will live alone
  In all our hearts, as mournful light
That broods above the fallen sun,
  And dwells in heaven half the night."

Second characteristic—Tennyson's wide sympathy. We come now to the almost inexhaustible question of Tennyson's variety of subject. Here, if you will glance at the immense scope of his works, written on different questions, you will start with amazement at the comprehensiveness—at the versatility, of the man who could write "Maud," after treating the philosophic and scientific, as well as the religious and psychological problems, in the " In Memoriam;" then sound to their depth the peculiarities of the bucolic mind, in the "Northern Farmer;" scan the great Woman's Rights question, in the poem of "The Princess;" and analyse psychologically the state into which the human mind falls in extreme old age, in "The Grandmother;" and prove the prince of storytellers in the "Idylls of the King"—and how rare is the storytelling faculty, in prose or poetry, the reading public know to their cost; but the Idylls are more than interesting tales well told, for, couched in the frame-work of the past, those old tales of the Round Table positively teem with the thoughts and feelings of our modern times; they repeat our own life dramas, until all the people there seem drawn out of the past and brought very near to us, by the intimate way in which we find them animated like ourselves, with the same hopes, and fears, and aspirations—and lastly, a man who in later life can pass easily to the creation of dramas, such as "Queen Mary," and "Harold," and "A'Beckett," and, after a comparatively brief study, seize those historical scenes and persons with a vigour of grip which might well make the despair of a Macaulay, a Froude, or a John Richard Green;—such a poet is indeed highly characteristic, and intensely representative, of the nineteenth century.

Third characteristic—Tennyson's Moral and Religious Instincts. In dealing now with Tennyson's religious sensibility, I come first to Tennyson's imaginative hold over past religious phases of Christian thought and feeling, and I dwell upon his deeply spiritual view of those two eternally recurrent phenomena of human intellect and passion in religion, the asceticism of Stylites, the ecstasy of St. Agnes—the Christianity of the Wilderness and of the Convent.

The sympathetic exercise of the imagination which enables a man to live and move in alien atmospheres—to realize other men's notions of life, to see things through their eyes—is the power which will alone enable us to take a wide interest in the condition of others, or to do justice to their religious, political, and social views when differing from our own.

It is just for want of seeing how people come to think and feel thus and thus, that sectarians in Church and State bite and devour one another. No one can understand his neighbour's creed without a certain exercise of imagination; and had we a little more of this faculty we should be able to live more calmly with Roman Catholics, dissenters, and other people who hold diverse opinions. And the moral lesson of a great imaginative effort like the poem of St. Simeon Stylites is—put yourself in his mental atmosphere, live in his age.

VI. THE CHRISTIANITY OF THE WILDERNESS —St. Simeon Stylites. If there is one thing more puzzling than another to the mind of an ordinary Englishman, it is the asceticism which prevailed in the primitive church. We ask, why did these men leave their comfort and their city life, to wander about in the wilderness in hunger and thirst and nakedness, living in dens and caves, and inflicting ceaseless self-torment? They went out from the great cities, such as Alexandria, or Rome, and mortified their bodies with fasting and prayer, until they became *Saints*, and people flocked from all quarters to see them, and finally worshipped them as half divine; and all this was at its height in the fourth and fifth centuries, and it is no little puzzle to some of us. The poem of which I am about to read a portion is that of St. Simeon Stylites, the prince of ascetics, who, because he could not sufficiently mortify his body by hunger and wandering, got on to the top of a pillar and lived there. There he stopped, and would come down only to mount a higher pillar, where he remained three years. The people crowded out to see him and bring him food; and thus he remained, exposed to all the inclemencies of the weather, preaching to the crowds, falling sometimes into long trances, until his fame spread as the greatest worker of miracles and the greatest saint in Christendom! One day he seemed to have been still for a longer time than usual. He was in the habit of bowing his head down to his knees, and he had not bowed himself for a long time. A devotee once counted that he bowed himself 1250 times, and then he left off counting. But when he had been now long motionless they climbed up to see what was the matter with him, and found he had been dead for some time!

Now, without realizing by the imagination, that age and atmosphere, it is impossible for us to understand how such conduct could commend itself to the multitude, or why they reckoned the ascetic a saint. But were you a poet, like Tennyson, you would seize the truth enshrined. Look at what Alexandria, Antioch, and the whole East was at that time. It was an age of gigantic crime, luxury, lawlessness, and selfishness; an age too of prodigies, superstitions, and portents; and if a man wanted to go right, he had to turn his back on the cities, and fly to the deserts. It was an age in which a man could hardly believe in the mastery of the soul over the body; and he who did believe, was constrained to sum up his belief in some immense symbol—nay, to become himself that symbol, as did Simeon upon his pillar. That spectacle meant—there is something in man that is greater than his body, that can master and even extinguish all its natural hunger and appetite—this body, which is always getting in the way of soul-progress! As the saint looked around, he saw men swept away by their bodily lusts, and ruled by all things which are transitory and ephemeral; and if, in the old days of Alexandria and Rome you would be a saint, surely you must get away from all that external world—mortify yourself, and treat every motion of the flesh as if it were a temptation of the devil! Thus you would at last have brought yourself into a state in which you were all spirit, and seemed lifted into a kind of supersensuous atmosphere above the world. That was, in exaggerated terms, in the language of a tremendous reaction, the simple announcement of the spiritual part of man's nature, the solitary supremacy of the soul! And it is as true now as then. Yes, there is something in man which is able to triumph over the body, which is able to keep in subordination the empire of the flesh; something which makes a man strong to put aside the blandishments of present delight, to come boldly to the Calvary of pain and grief, and lay down his life there with Christ. Unless you have got some of this power you are not fit for much in time or in eternity; unless you can subdue your appetites to noble ends, and walk straight on in the path of duty, cost what it may, and do this through the years, you are not worthy to be His disciple whom St. Simeon Stylites stood and witnessed for in the wilderness!

Before approaching that pillar of agony and ecstasy you must understand that far back age. The unscrupulous bishops; the massacres of the monks by the people, of the people by the monks; the games of the bloody arena; the violence and licentiousness of the emperors; the public atheism and demoralization; the universal corruption. Then, in the spirit of St. Simeon Stylites, turn your back on that evil and perverse generation, deaf alike to entreaty and menace, and fly for your life to the wilderness, and show that there is still some power in man which can afford to despise all the ambitions, pleasures, and degrading follies of the flesh. Let me read to you some of that strange rhapsody in which the man's mind sometimes seems to give way; and it is quite evident that at certain points he is wandering, at other times he sinks into simple weakness and despondency; then he sees visions, and is lifted into ecstasy. But all through he holds on consistently to the great moral and spiritual truth which is at the bottom of his good confession; and just at the hour of his death you will see how he returns to perfect clearness and calmness, and holds up on high, above all the confusion and turmoil, the spiritual truth which has been proclaimed and set forth amidst the hallucinations of the mystic.

> "Although I be the basest of mankind,
> From scalp to sole one slough and crust of sin,
> Unfit for earth, unfit for heaven, scarce meet

> For troops of devils mad with blasphemy,
> I will not cease to grasp the hope I hold
> Of saintdom, and to clamour, mourn, and sob,
> Battering the gates of heaven with storms of prayer,—
> Have mercy, Lord, and take away my sin."

Then he begins to recount all his sufferings, and at last, in order to be more alone with God,

> "Three years I lived upon a pillar, high
> Six cubits, and three years on one of twelve;
> And twice three years I crouched on one that rose
> Twenty by measure; last of all I grew
> Twice ten long weary weary years to this,
> That numbers forty cubits from the soil."

And now comes on his soul the ever-recurrent agony for the sinfulness of his nature. Every pain of his chafing body, and every resistance to the torture which he is undergoing, seems to him to be but another sign of the wretched depravity of his flesh; and after giving way to a fit of contrition for what he calls his "miserable sins," he addresses the crowd at his feet. After a long and bitter burst of emotion the mood of self-reproach is exhausted, and he turns to the people in a soberer strain, which soon yields to the semi-prophetic elation of the miracle worker.

"Good people, you do ill to kneel to me.
What is it I can have done to merit this?
I am a sinner viler than you all.
It may be I have wrought some miracles,
And cured some halt and maim'd; but what of that?
It may be no one, even among the saints,
May match his pains with mine; but what of that?
Yet do not rise; for you may look on me,
And in your looking you may kneel to God.
Speak! is there any of you halt or maim'd?
I think you know I have some power with heaven,
From my long penance; let him speak his wish.
Yes, I can heal him. Power goes forth from me,
They say that they are heal'd. Ah, hark! they shout
'St. Simeon Stylites.'"

Then he begins to recount his own method of dealing with sin to the people.

"O my sons, my sons,
I, Simeon of the pillar, by surname
Stylites among men; I, Simeon,
The watcher on the column till the end;
I, Simeon, whose brain the sunshine bakes;
I, whose bald brows in silent hours become
Unnaturally hoar with rime, do now,
From my high nest of penance here, proclaim
That Pontius and Iscariot by my side
Show'd like fair seraphs. On the coals I lay,
A vessel full of sin; all hell beneath
Made me boil over. Devils pluck'd my sleeve
Abaddon and Asmodeus caught at me;
I smote them with the cross.

* * * * *
       Mortify
Your flesh, like me, with scourges and with thorns;
Smite, shrink not, spare not. It may be, fast
Whole Lents, and pray. I hardly, with slow steps—
With slow, faint steps, and much exceeding pain,
Have scrambled past those pits of fire that still
Sing in mine ears. But yield not me the praise.
God only through His bounty hath thought fit,
Among the powers and princes of this world,
To make me an example to mankind,
Which few can reach to. Yet I do not say
But that a time may come—yea, even now,
Now, now, his footsteps smite the threshold stairs
Of life—I say, that time is at the doors
When you may worship me without reproach;
For I will leave my relics in your land,
And you may carve a shrine about my dust,
And burn a fragrant lamp before my bones,
When I am gathered to the glorious saints."

Then, after another crisis of feeling, approaching at the end to ecstasy, he goes on—

"Speak, if there be a priest, a man of God,
 Among you there, and let him presently
 Approach, and lean a ladder on the shaft,
 And, climbing up into my airy home,
 Deliver me the blessed sacrament;
 For by the warning of the Holy Ghost
 I prophecy that I shall die to-night,
 A quarter before twelve.

> But Thou, O Lord,
> Aid all this foolish people; let them take
> Example, pattern; lead them to Thy light."

His death is quite calm, quite collected. Note how with his latest breath returns the greatest, sanest expression of the spiritual life to which he bears witness.

VII. THE CHRISTIANITY OF THE CONVENT—ST. AGNES.

I pass, in conclusion, to the best and purest type of conventual asceticism, in the gentle piety of St. Agnes.

Once more we find reflected in this clear image eternally recurrent states of the soul. We too meditate like St. Agnes; our meditation rises into prayer, our prayer again rises into an atmosphere which cannot be described; in it we seem like St. Paul to be lifted into heaven, hearing words which it is not lawful or possible to utter—those blessed moments which Robertson calls the very "bridal hours of the soul," when we get strength and refreshment to return to the world, to go on with the daily drudgeries of life. How quiet is her image, how pure her soul, as she stands looking out dreamily on to the fair expanse of moonlit snow. Note how her calm thoughts flow naturally into prayer, which in its turn broadens into fuller life, as she rises at last out of meditation and prayer, and is lifted up into the imaginative ecstasy of the rushing and glowing close. The whole poem is a most beautiful example of the convent piety of the Middle Ages; and although it may to some extent be out of the range of our modern taste, yet it has the elements of truth in it, and is genuinely and everlastingly illustrative of the elements of human character and the experiences of the spiritual life:—

> "Deep on the convent roof the snows
>   Are sparkling to the moon:
> My breath to heaven like vapour goes:
>   May my soul follow soon!
> The shadows of the convent towers
>   Slant down the snowy sward,
> Still creeping with the creeping hours
>   That lead me to my Lord:
> Make Thou my spirit pure and clear
>   As are the frosty skies,
> Or this first snowdrop of the year
>   That in my bosom lies."

The second verse also begins in meditation and ends in prayer, but the last verse rises out of prayer into ecstasy.

"He lifts me to the golden doors;
   The flashes come and go;
All heaven bursts her starry floors,
   And strows her lights below,
And deepens on and up! The gates
   Roll back, and far within
For me the Heavenly Bridegroom waits,
   To make me pure of sin.
The sabbaths of Eternity,
   One sabbath deep and wide—
A light upon the shining sea—
   The Bridegroom with His bride."

III.

Tennyson.

THE VISION OF SIN, AND THE PALACE OF ART.

III.

Tennyson.

THE VISION OF SIN, AND THE PALACE OF ART.

DEVELOP further to-night Tennyson's third characteristic, Moral and Religious Sensibility. Teaching by allegory has ever been a favourite practice with prophet and poet; but before I select the two great Tennysonian allegories of the "Vision of Sin," and the "Palace of Art," I must call your attention to that conception or theory of human nature on which they are based.

We are held to be tripartite—body, mind, and spirit. Man is not a mere animal or body; not a mere calculating machine, or intellect; not a mere spirit, independent of either. He is tripartite unity.

We have just seen, in St. Simeon Stylites, and St. Agnes, the attempt of ascetic and conventual Christianity to isolate the spirit, to crush the body and ignore the mind; we now come with the "Vision of Sin" upon man's attempt to live merely as a thing of body, ignoring both intellect and soul. Of course such presentations of life are ideal; no one can utterly and consistently ignore all but one side; we are too cunningly made for that; still there is the tendency, and here in this tremendous allegory of the "Vision of Sin," the poet embodies that tendency, showing the sensual youth, the degraded old age, and while pointing to the terrible Nemesis manifest to all, reverently suspending the sentence upon each. All through we cannot forget that man is a being of common sense and common reason; yet we have before us the future of a man who throws aside all this, and delights only in what he can touch, and taste, and see. Gratification of the senses, and the luxurious moment—the nerve dissolving melody, followed by "the cold heavy hueless vapour" of reaction—the apathy, dissipation, and wreck of the whole man; all this is made to pass before us in a series of vivid and poetical cartoons; immense human pleasure, and passion, and suffering—and brooding over all the sad Nemesis of the senses. And as I look around me I see the giddy way in which the men and women—not only of this age, but of every age—hurry on and on after pleasure, without thinking of the consequences;

seizing one butterfly after another; never asking of the appetites what they were really meant for, how they should be used, what may be their right proportion in the general economy of human life, or what the duty of providing pleasure for others; but dead, wrapt up in self—the lowest self; eat, drink, smoke, sleep—until the blood thickens, and the nerves rot with indulgence in every kind of licentious living. Is this one side of our age? Mark how men drain every cup of pleasure, until sensibility wears out; and then health wears out; and then ability to feel wears out. Give me the poet or teacher who will put a true picture of this before men; and he shall do the age golden service. Well, what if this " Vision of Sin " be an ideal picture, isolating one side of man! let us admit that man is never wholly like what one side of himself may become. What if, because you are spiritually constituted, you will be ever haunted with the overtones of the soul—still let the allegory of Sin pass before you as an embodied tendency.

I. THE VISION OF SIN.—There rises before us the image of a man, glowing with health and youth, eager for all that these alone can bestow, riding a winged horse, the horse being his own soul; but he weighs down that Pegasus with the dull leaden weight of his own sensual personality. The soul within him frets and chafes—struggling, impatient, restless—yet plods on, but with slow and flagging paces. Such an one is put before us, approaching the palace gates of Pleasure. Then follow the revels —and then comes an awful pause of meditation— and then the lapse of time; and when the curtain is raised again we see the same figure—yet not the same, for it is one over whom the tide of years has rolled, over whom the wearing storm of passion has swept, and left its victim to a miserable, drivelling, degraded, incapable old age. And so these two pictures are put before you, and the solemn verdict is reverently suspended; and the highest flight of the poet and teacher is reached in this reverent suspension of judgment.

The poem opens:—

"I had a vision when the night was late:
A youth came riding toward a palace-gate;
He rode a horse with wings, that would have flown,
But that his heavy rider kept him down."

Let us throw a veil over the wild revel in the halls of sensual delight. The poet is suddenly rapt away in contemplation: the maddening giddy dance, the delirious groups, are shut out; and we seem to move aside, and look upon the eternal outcome of all these things: we see the consequences inexorably working out; we see the great moral tides as they ebb and flow through the ages. The poet stands in the midst of a solemn landscape, and, absorbed in the contemplation of eternal principles, he marks the great tide, as of recording fate, like a thick hueless vapour, floating on and on towards him, from the still heights:

> "And then I look'd up toward a mountain tract,
> That girt the region with high cliff and lawn:
> I saw that every morning, far withdrawn
> Beyond the darkness and the cataract,
> God made Himself an awful rose of dawn,
> Unheeded: and detaching, fold by fold,
> From those still heights, and slowly drawing near,
> A vapour—heavy, hueless, formless, cold—
> Came floating on, for many a month and year,
> Unheeded: and I thought I would have spoken,
> And warn'd that madman ere it grew too late:
> But as in dreams, I could not. Mine was broken.
> When that cold vapour touch'd the palace-gate,
> And link'd again—"

When the prophetic vision is resumed, the same figure, and yet not the same, is before us:

> "I saw, within my head,
> A gray and gap-tooth'd man, as lean as Death,
> Who slowly rode across a wither'd heath,
> And 'lighted at a ruin'd inn."

Note the careful contrast: instead of the young man, a "gray and gap-tooth'd man;" instead of one in the bloom of youth, a man "as lean as Death;" instead of a noble courser with wings, he slowly rides a miserable worn-out hack; and instead of arriving at a "palace gate," he came to a "ruin'd inn," and said,—

> "Wrinkled ostler, grim and thin!
> Here is custom come your way;
> Take my brute, and lead him in;
> Stuff his ribs with mouldy hay."

Next we perceive his loss of belief—not only in friendship and human love, but in all the great social and political virtues; all has gone down in the great charnel-house of ruined appetites, and the man has lost faith in everything worth living for.

Then follow the ghastly pleasantry, and the free cynical rant of a worn-out sensualist, tottering, with gibe and semi-drunken maunder, on the brink of the grave. Having lost all self-respect, he mixes as an equal with the lowest tipplers; having lost all religion, he mocks at any chance phrase of theology that he can recollect; sneers at friendship, love, virtue; denounces as delusive all social and political aspirations—freedom, reform, 'tis all one—

> " Drink we last the public fool,
>   Frantic love, and frantic hate."

And even there as, he sits, his blood begins to chill; his fancies grow more pale and ghastly; the old skeleton hopes and fears, dead and horrid memories, come thronging like a troop of furies towards him: shall he greet them with awful tremblings, or wild delirium? Drink! drink to the end!

> " Trooping from their mouldy dens,
>   The chapfallen circle spreads:
> Welcome! fellow-citizens,
>   Hollow hearts and empty heads!
>   You are bones—and what of that?" &c.

But the last dull spark in his own old worn-out carcass is beginning to fade. A sort of feeble lethargy takes possession of brain and limb, against which he continues to fill the can, and struggle in vain; and looking at his companion, he sees the same torpor creeping over him:

> "Thou art mazed! the night is long,
> And the longer night is near."

And then, feeling the very chills of death beginning to come upon him, the wretched worn-out creature blurts forth, with a kind of vindictive scream of terror, and mad clinging to existence,

> "Dregs of life, and lees of man,
> Yet we will not die forlorn!"

As the voice grows faint the ghastly scene is rolled away like a scroll, and the poet finds himself once more contemplating the eternal results of inexorable and Divine principles. The moral teaching is emphasized in the three oracular utterances:

> "Behold, it was a crime
> Of sense avenged by sense, that wore with time!"

> "The crime of sense became
> The crime of malice, and is equal blame."

> "He had not wholly quench'd his power:
> A little grain of conscience made him sour."

Then comes a wild cry, beating to the heights—the cry of fallen despairing humanity, when the veil falls off, and all is seen in the hideous and naked deformity and ruin of sin.

> "Is there any hope?"

And with the truest deepest reverence the seer pauses to record—

> "An answer pealed from that high land,
> But in a tongue no man could understand.
> And on the glittering limit, far withdrawn,
> God made Himself an awful rose of dawn.

So we must leave them—the frail, the tempted, the sinful ones alone—with their God. Still the Vision of Sin haunts us! that awful spectacle of shattered sensibilities—lost, wasted capacities—Divine instincts smothered—all that makes life worth living trampled under foot; and as we contemplate them closely—the awful Nemesis of lust, and the collapse of the whole spiritual fabric—might we not involuntarily cry out, like Balaam, "May I die the death of the righteous, and may my last end be like his?"

II. THE PALACE OF ART.—Here you have the isolation of another side of human nature. This time it is the intellectual side—that of the man who lives entirely for culture. You have seen what became of the merely sensual man; now we are to contemplate the merely intellectual man. This selfish, solitary, isolation of self-culture is a besetting tendency of the age, both in art and literature; to cultivate everything for selfish enjoyment; to ignore the rights, the feelings, the sympathies of others; to forget that they have any claims upon us. The fair scenes of earth, the religions of the world, the wise and great, the seers of the age—all are to be pressed into the service of intellectual pleasure; but the great lesson of human life—the training, through human sympathy, grief, helpfulness, and manly endeavour, for eternity—this is missed; nothing is allowed to bring home its deeper teaching; everything is used for pleasure—pleasure more than animal—intellectual, imaginative—but at best selfish, isolated; and this course also leads to despair, disappointment, and misery.

Practically no human being can do what is supposed to be done in the poem. It is again the tendency that is dealt with. Just as no man can live for his body alone until he becomes a mere driveller in *delirium tremens*, so no man can live for his mind alone. In neither case can he wholly quench his power; "a little grain of conscience makes him sour."

You may go along this road, living in your Palace of Art a life of selfishness and self-isolation, and enjoying your own happiness, without thinking or caring for that of others. This course Tennyson sketches, its progress and its inevitable fate—a fate written upon the page of history itself, in characters of fire and blood.

In Athens, sensuality and culture at their best—ended with the murder of Socrates; at their worst—in Nero's reign, with the Christian massacres and the fire of Rome. In this nineteenth century the same state of feeling is approached by men who despise the people, who narrow their sympathies to a small and confined æsthetic circle, whether in music, art, or science. The habit of mind is the same in all men who live solely for their own pleasure, who shut out as far as they can everything else from life, and deem themselves the princes of intellect, the cultured elect of the earth. For whom indeed need they care but for their own sweet selves? what else is worth caring about?

I warn you against this insidious tendency of our day to love and pamper self, to ignore and despise your fellow creatures *en masse*—the " people that are cursed, and know nothing." It is a narrow, selfish, mean policy; and upon it is pronounced a true verdict in this allegory of the "Palace of Art."

"I built my soul a lordly pleasure-house,
  Wherein at ease for aye to dwell.

I said, 'O soul, make merry and carouse,
    Dear soul, for all is well.'

A huge crag-platform, smooth as burnish'd brass,
    I chose. The rangèd ramparts bright
From level meadow bases, of deep grass,
    Suddenly seal'd the light.

Thereon I built it firm. Of ledge or shelf
    The rock rose clear, or winding stair.
My soul would live alone unto herself,
    In her high palace there.

And 'While the world runs round and round,' I said,
    ' Reign thou apart, a quiet king,—
Still as, while Saturn whirls, his steadfast shade
    Sleeps on his luminous ring.'

To which my soul made answer readily:
    ' Trust me, in bliss I shall abide
In this great mansion, that is built for me,
    So royal-rich and wide.' "

So then a palace is built, with every conceivable beauty of architecture; and inwardly it is equally adorned :

" Full of great rooms and small the palace stood,
    All various, each a perfect whole
From living Nature, fit for every mood
    And change of my still soul."

But in all this the " still soul " finds no spiritual

meaning. For it there is nothing beneath the surface of life. To the loving heart all this world's beauty and grace is filled with fair and heavenly images, fit to draw the heart nearer to man because nearer to God. Not so in the Palace of Art; here man only looked at the things which were for himself, which promised immediate entertainment, and solace for his transient fancy.

Ah! there was one whom the cloudy summer morn reminded of those whose "goodness was as a morning cloud, and as the early dew that vanished away" (Hos. vi. 4). Another, when he saw the sun unfailing in the regularity of his course, exclaimed, "His compassions fail not; they are new every morning" (Lam. iii. 22). The spring reminded David of the heart of an upright ruler: "He that ruleth over men must be just, ruling in the fear of God; and he shall be as the light of the morning when the sun riseth, even a morning without cloud, as the tender grass springing out of the earth by clear shining after rain " (2 Sam. xxiii. 3, 4).

To the Psalmist, the vision of "a tract of barren sand," which in the "Palace of Art" is a mere imaginative freak, was a symbol of the soul without God:

"in a barren and dry land, where no water is." To the Prophet "an iron coast and angry waves, you seemed to hear them climb and fall," told of the " wicked who were like a troubled sea, that could not rest."

To David, "a full-fed river, winding slow by herds upon an endless plain," gave the sweet promise, "They shall drink of the pleasures as out of a river;" whilst "the reapers at their sultry toil" told of those who had sown in tears, but should " doubtless come again with rejoicing, and bringing their sheaves with them."

But all these fair symbols in the Palace of Art did but reflect back to the man his own selfish spirit. His eyes were fast sealed to the opening revelations of God's many-sided world. And as the outward scenes of earth passed before him, mere idle or amusing visions, so did he pass in review the forms of faith, and the great religions of the world. For a moment the Roman Catholic Faith smiled to him, with its—

> " Maid-mother by a crucifix,
> In tracts of pasture sunny warm."

In that fair symbol there was no deeper teaching, no lesson of history, or feeling of universal interest and significance. It was simply "the maid-mother by a crucifix"—a very pretty and pleasant thing for you to have in your room, of which to say how fairly it is painted, or how well the anatomy is studied, or how "nicely felt" and harmonious the colouring. No pathetic memory of the time when to the devout heart the love of the Virgin was all in all; when mediæval theology had turned God into a despot seeking vengeance, and Christ into the victim upon whom the Divine fury was exhausted, and thus left to man a terror in place of a Father—a sacrificial victim instead of a friend. Then "the maid-mother with the crucifix" took, indeed, in popular theology the place of her Son, who had been thrust beyond the region of human friendship, for she thus summed up in herself the human loving side of God, and restored to religious contemplation that indispensable element of Christian devotion. But of all this no faint perception in the Palace of Art.

As a caprice of the mind, the Mahomedan religion next had its turn, as—

> "Thronging all one porch of Paradise,
> A group of houris bow'd to see
> The dying Islamite, with hands and eyes
> That said, 'We wait for thee.'"

There was something beautiful about the group of houris bowing to see the dying Islamite; but it was a mere image, which struck upon the superficial sense; this self-centred and self-satisfied epicurean smiled approvingly on houri and Islamite alike. But he who looked rightly upon Mahomedanism, would have seized with emotion its central truth of the one great God. The Palace of Art could only make room for the lowest and most sensual aspect of Mahomedanism—the Paradise, and the Houri.

The great religions of Greece and of Rome next pass before him; but how? They come robbed of their old vitality; no more the faith of a worshipping people who seemed to see a Deity everywhere—in the woods, the rivers, the skies, the seas, filled with youth and Divine life. To this earth-encrusted spirit the meaner, grosser aspects of Greek religion alone offered themselves naturally. The excesses of the gods:

> "Europa's mantle blew unclasp'd,
> From off her shoulder backward borne."

Or else:

> "Flush'd Ganymede, his rosy thigh
> Half buried in the Eagle's down."

Alas! if Greek and Roman religion could teach us no more than this! So, after exhausting in its own vampire way the fair scenes and religions of the world, the very seers of the ages have now to be pressed into this fruitless barren service of a barren soul. So,

> "With choice paintings of wise men I hung
> The royal dais round.
> For there was Milton, like a seraph strong;
> Beside him Shakespeare, bland and mild;
> And there the world-worn Dante grasp'd his song,
> And somewhat grimly smiled."

And in this noble assembly, dumb oracles to deaf ears, the soul sat herself down on her throne at last. Then comes the song of the soul, as she sings to her own secret isolated self in her Palace of Art:

> "She sat betwixt the shining oriels,
> To sing her songs alone.
> Singing and murmuring in her feastful mirth,
> Joying to feel herself alive,
> Lord over nature, lord of the visible earth,
> Lord of the senses five;
> Communing with herself: 'All these are mine;
> And let the world have peace or wars,
> 'Tis one to me.'"

To this habit of mind all the rest of the world is entire dross. The sense of moral responsibility is gone. What care you for the suffering, toiling millions! No thought of ameliorating or soothing by attempting to enter into their sufferings; they are only so many—

> " Darkening droves of swine
>   That range on yonder plain,"

And may they never come any nearer! so saith the soul from her Palace of Art.

> " And so she throve and prosper'd: so three years
>   She prosper'd: on the fourth she fell,
> Like Herod, when the shout was in his ears,
>   Struck through with pangs of hell.
>
> Lest she should fail and perish utterly,
>   God, before whom ever lie bare
> The abysmal depths of Personality,
>   Plagued her with sore despair.
>
> *　　*　　*　　*　　*
>
> Deep dread, and loathing of her solitude,
>   Fell on her; from which mood was born
> Scorn of herself; again, from out that mood,
>   Laughter at her self-scorn.
>
> 'What! is not this my place of strength,' she said,
>   My spacious mansion built for me,
> Whereof the strong foundation stones were laid
>   Since my first memory?'
>
> *　　*　　*　　*　　*

So when four years were wholly finishèd
　　She threw her royal robes away;
'Make me a cottage in the vale,' she said,
　　'Where I may mourn and pray.

Yet pull not down my palace towers that are
　　So lightly, beautifully built:
Perchance I may return with others there
　　When I have purged my guilt.'"

So, you see after all, the healthy instincts are bound to triumph at last; the soul must get back to nature out of herself, her isolation—her selfish isolation, and learn to help others in their lonely suffering. And when the lesson of humanity is learned, and not before, the lesson of art is wholesome; then you may return with others there: but the guilt of selfishness and spiritual isolation must first be purged; man and nature must bind us to God.

Great allegories these, of life and sin, but not of despair. I have now followed, with the poet as my teacher, the three sides of human isolation, summed up in three separate visions. The first and noblest shows the tendency to believe that we are all soul, and to ignore the bodily vehicle of soul—so fearfully and wonderfully made, so intimately married to it. Whether this culminate in the religion of the solitary pillar or the secluded convent, it is false. The second error lies in supposing that you are merely a sensual being, and that you can be happy solely in the gratification of your body. The third fallacy is to think that you are merely intellectual and not spiritual, and that you can live for ever in a Palace of Art.

It remains for us to knit together these three sides of human nature, and to this Tennyson will guide us in " In Memoriam." There the whole man is displayed in right proportion—body, mind, and spirit. All three, seen before as disjointed and one-sided manifestations, are there welded together into one perfect whole. Man rises, in body, mind, and spirit, into the glorious liberty of a child of God, and is seen aspiring to something like "the measure of the stature of the fulness of Christ."

IV.
Tennyson.
IN MEMORIAM.

IV.

Tennyson.

IN MEMORIAM.

E have seen in the asceticism of Stylites, and in the conventual devotion and ecstasy of St. Agnes, what becomes of human nature when considered as nothing but spirit. We have noted the wreck of the body, and the overthrow of the mind. We have seen in the "Vision of Sin" what became of human nature regarded simply as body: the worship of the senses was shown to be, not only the wreck of the body, but the palsy of the soul and the paralysis of the intellect. We have seen in the "Palace of Art" what became of the culture of the body and the mind—the life of the senses, the intellect, and the imagination, apart from the spirit; we noted how nearly the spirit succumbed to that treatment; we assisted at the desperate struggle. But it remained for us to learn what human nature might be when treated as St. Paul

treats it, in body, mind, and spirit. The isolated elements combine at last to make the whole man—the sublime humanity as conceived by God—like God Himself, tripartite and triune.

This is the lesson of the " In Memoriam:" the developed humanity stands forth at last, disciplined by loss, purified by suffering, and lifted up into heavenly places through the earth-born love.

In the " In Memoriam " you have a man who thrills and kindles to all outward impressions; his senses are keenly alive to every change of the seasons, to all external nature, to every pulse of pleasure and pain; his mind is alert—" who loves not knowledge? who shall rail against her beauty?" his affections are active—they cannot always acquiesce in purely intellectual speculation, the heart stands up and answers, "I have felt;" and above all there is the brooding sense of the infinite mystery about us, and the longing for the infinite love, and the inspired eye which looks through nature up to nature's God—that God who ever lives and loves—" one God, one law, one element, and one far off Divine event, to which the whole creation moves."

Now the key-note of this great poem is sorrow—sorrow coming out of the shadow of a great loss; and the atmosphere of sorrow is just the atmosphere in which it is the most instructive to study human nature. Do you want to know about the body? It is not best to study it in a state of health, but when it is diseased. Doctors will tell you *that* is the time to make discoveries and experiments, and to add permanently to our understanding of the human framework; and indeed, most of our medical knowledge is derived not merely from morbid anatomy, but from the diagnosis of various diseases—not the monotonous chronicle of healthy days and nights. And to prove a man, you must find him out in seasons of sorrow and pain: how does he bear it, how does he act? And a man who will note such an experience adds to our stock of knowledge, and thought, and feeling; he is a teacher, and his book is the book of nature, and of life. And what he does for one he does for all: one man's inner life is really a thousand inner lives; he reads them the open secrets of their hearts, by showing them his own; he and they are no longer solitary units, but are seen, in a great work of art—a picture or a poem—to have universal elements, to belong to a whole. That is why we listen with wrapt attention to him "who sings to one clear harp in divers tones." And the tones of sorrow invariably arrest; they are of profound and general interest; they draw us in spite of ourselves; they win us and cling to us—because they reflect some of the deepest and most universal aspects of our common humanity. That is why Jesus Christ, who was "a man of sorrows," stands for ever by the wayside in the great thoroughfares of time, saying, "Behold and see, if there is any sorrow like unto my sorrow." And because he was "a man of sorrows, and acquainted with grief," therefore he could say, "Come unto me, all ye that labour and are heavy laden, and I will give you rest."

Sorrow, as W. F. Robertson has remarked, acts very differently upon different constitutions. It is like fire—it melts some like wax, and hardens others like clay; it sifts a man's heart, it finds out weaknesses, it tries him like gold; and that is its best work. The fire of tribulation has often a great cleansing and purifying effect; it wakes up a man's inner life, smelts the dross out of him, leaving him pure gold. And the work of sorrow was never shown so noble and so complete as in this great poem of "In Memoriam."

The circumstances from which it sprang are probably known to every one here present. Alfred Tennyson, in his youth, formed a very close friendship with Arthur Hallam, son of the great historian Henry Hallam. The Hallams at that time lived in Wimpole Street; the historian and his son used to sit in this church of St. James, Westmoreland Street, in a pew just behind the first pillar, about forty-five years ago; and it is a curious incident, that the first time I saw Alfred Tennyson, in this church not very long ago, he was sitting, with his son Hallam Tennyson, almost in the same place.

In the early Autumn of 1833, Arthur Hallam went abroad: on the 16th of September, at Vienna, a sudden rush of blood to the head, put an instantaneous end to his life. "God's finger touched him, and he slept." On the 3rd of January, 1834, he was buried in the chancel of the church at Clevedon, on the Severn. Tennyson's whole soul seems to have been wrapped up in this early affection. For a time he seems to have been almost paralyzed with sorrow; and when the heavy cloud began to lift, out of the great calamity came those tender voices of passion, despair, remonstrance, and hope, which have comforted so many forlorn spirits, and are perhaps destined to be Tennyson's most precious legacy to posterity.

The opening of the "In Memoriam," and its close, are like the calm deep sea water. We go from a noble port of peace, across a stormy restless ocean, and we come at last to the shining coast, to the fair haven of the soul, to the eternal rest.

Although the "In Memoriam" is full of wild cries, doubts, difficulties, and sorrows, it begins, as it ends, with a triumphant strain of praise:

>"Strong Son of God, immortal Love,
>>Whom we, that have not seen Thy face,
>>By faith, and faith alone, embrace,
>Believing where we cannot prove;
>
>Thine are these orbs of light and shade;
>>Thou madest life in man and brute;
>>Thou madest Death; and lo, Thy foot
>Is on the skull which Thou hast made.
>
>Thou wilt not leave us in the dust:
>>Thou madest man, he knows not why;
>>He thinks he was not made to die;
>And Thou hast made him: Thou art just.

*　　*　　*　　*　　*

> Forgive these wild and wandering cries,
>   Confusions of a wasted youth;
>   Forgive them where they fail in truth,
> And in Thy wisdom make me wise.

Some old Father of the Church says, that every human life may be divided into four periods. The first period is that one in which a man is overcome without a struggle; the second period is that in which a man struggles, but is overcome; the third is that one in which a man struggles and overcomes; and the fourth is a period of peace. Those divisions may be applied to the psychology of the "In Memoriam." It is the story of, 1st, sorrow unopposed; 2nd, sorrow opposed; 3rd, sorrow conquered; 4th, peace. Of course, as these phases run into each other the divisions must not be too closely pressed, although I have marked them at certain stanzas.

I. SORROW UNOPPOSED.—All through the long first period, running from the 1st to the 55th stanza, certainly we have the spectacle of a mind tossed about on an uneasy sea of sorrow. At first, Sorrow seems to be accepted as his natural companion, though her's is "a cruel fellowship," and she a

"Priestess in the halls of Death." The world seems like a dream, and

> "Nature like a phantom stands,
> With all the music in her tone,
> A hollow echo of our own—
> A hollow form, with empty hands."

He walks abroad: he gets no comfort from outward nature. Just as you or I may have looked up to the silent stars, and gazed upon the glory of the summer fields, and have had to feel as if they mocked us. All joy seems to have been taken out of the world, when grief is too heavy and loss too recent.

Slowly the ministry of nature begins, by reflecting his moods; for "he sees himself in all he sees." But the saddest aspects alone arrest him: in the churchyard, the old yew netting its fibres about the dreamless head; or "from waste places comes a cry, and murmurs from the dying sun." For him no cheerful strain streams from the earthly paradise of summer; but the dove sings her dolorous message. The winds wail sadly; Autumn comes, and "the last red leaf is whirled away," and "the rooks are blown about the skies," till at last the pressure of outward nature is almost too much for him:

> "I scarce could brook the strain and stir
> Which make the barren branches bound."

And the nearest approach to solace comes to him in the peace and silence of the lonely Autumn mornings, on the wild heath:

> "Calm and deep peace in this wide air,
> These leaves that redden to the fall;
> And in my heart, if calm at all,
> The calmness of a calm despair."

The usual letters of condolence arrive:

> "One writes that 'Other friends remain,'
> That 'Loss is common to the race,'—
> And common is the common-place,
> And vacant chaff, well meant for grain."

But his heart is elsewhere. In imagination he traverses distant waters, and reaches the ship coming homewards with its sad freight, the body of his friend:

> "I hear the noise about the keel;
> I hear the bell struck in the night;
> I see the cabin window bright;
> I see the sailor at the wheel."

At last the ship enters English waters, and the transference of his friend's body from foreign to English soil is memorialized in these exquisite lines:—

> "The Danube to the Severn gave
> The darken'd heart that beat no more;
> They laid him by the pleasant shore,
> And in the hearing of the wave.

> There twice a day the Severn fills;
>   The salt sea-water passes by,
>   And hushes half the babbling Wye,
> And makes a silence in the hills.
>
> The Wye is hush'd, nor moved along,—
>   And hush'd my deepest grief of all,
>   When, fill'd with tears that cannot fall,
> I brim with sorrow-drowning song.
>
> The tide flows down, the wave again
>   Is vocal in its wooded walls;
>   My deeper anguish also falls,
> And I can speak a little then."

Nothing is now left but memory.

> "The path by which we twain did go,
>   Which led by tracts that pleased us well,
>   Thro' four sweet years arose and fell,
> From flower to flower, from snow to snow.
>
> And we with singing cheer'd the way;
>   And, crown'd with all the season lent,
>   From April on to April went,
> And glad at heart from May to May.
>
> But where the path we walk'd began
>   To slant the fifth Autumnal slope,
>   As we descended, following Hope,
> There sat the Shadow fear'd of man,—
>
> Who broke our fair companionship,
>   And spread his mantle, dark and cold,
>   And wrapt thee formless in the fold,
> And dull'd the murmur on thy lip,—

And bore thee where I could not see,
  Nor follow, though I walk in haste,
  And think that, somewhere in the waste,
The Shadow sits and waits for me."

So months rolled on, and Christmas came—a sad anniversary for many who have lost dear friends. They may try the old pastimes, and the old songs; but the joy has faded out of life, and now it is pain that binds heart to heart, as once it was joy. But the memory of the dead seems to lift them up to a higher level, and their hearts are raised for a moment beyond the clouds of sorrow and death, into the heaven of consolation and peace:

" We paused: the winds were in the beech:
  We heard them sweep the winter land;
  And in a circle hand in hand
Sat silent, looking each at each.

Then echo-like our voices rang;
  We sang, tho' every eye was dim,
  A merry song we sang with him
Last year; impetuously we sang.

We ceased: a gentler feeling crept
  Upon us: surely rest is meet.
  'They rest,' we said; 'their rest is sweet,'—
And silence follow'd, and we wept.

> Our voices took a higher range;
>   Once more we sang: 'They do not die,
>   Nor lose their mortal sympathy,
> Nor change to us, although they change;
>
> Rapt from the fickle and the frail,
>   With gather'd power, yet the same,
>   Pierces the keen seraphic flame
> From orb to orb, from veil to veil.'"

So passes the first Christmas; and as life resumes its usual tenour, and the shock of grief subsides, the mind awakes to those unquiet speculations which force themselves upon us from time to time, as we contemplate the mystery of Death. "Where is the spirit? What is the spirit doing?"—the old questions, which will not die, come back, again and again. Perhaps his friend has ceased to be! perhaps if he exists he will be for ever out of reach! a—

> "Spectral doubt, which makes me cold—
> That I shall be thy mate no more.
> Tho' following with an upward mind
>   The wonders that have come to thee,
>   Thro' all the secular to be,—
> But evermore a life behind."

So those who have gone before seem to have stolen a march upon us, and perhaps we shall never be able to overtake them! Another speculation then comes: perhaps the life of the soul is suspended in sleep, so that when the body lies in the grave the spirit also sleeps—until the fulness of time, when life shall come back, and love survive! Joyful anticipation! Nothing of the bitter past shall stain the long harmonious years; only, perchance, some shadows of remembrance left, some dim touch of earthly things. But this thought is in its turn clouded over by the old haunting notion of the Nirwana: perhaps we shall be merged in the ocean of Being, all individuality lost. But no; each being has been rounded to a separate mind; his isolation grows defined, and for ever! Eagerly he gropes about, but all in vain, for a proof, a hint, a suggestion, that it is so; and his weary spirit at last exhales its sorrow, its longing, and its fatigue, in prayer:

> "Be near me when my light is low,
>   When the blood creeps, and the nerves prick
>   And tingle, and the heart is sick,
> And all the wheels of Being slow.
> Be near me when the sensuous frame
>   Is rack'd with pangs that conquer trust;
>   And Time, a maniac scattering dust;
> And Life, a Fury slinging flame.
> Be near me when my faith is dry,
>   And men the flies of latter spring,

> That lay their eggs, and sting, and sing,
> And weave their petty cells, and die.
> Be near me when I fade away,
> To point the term of human strife,
> And on the low dark verge of life
> The twilight of eternal day."

There is nothing left for the soul in its abyss of sorrow, but trust! infinite trust!

> "Behold, we know not anything;
> I can but trust that good shall fall
> At last—far off—at last, to all,
> And every winter change to spring."

But the glow of faith itself passes; that too was unstable and transitory; and the broken spirit relapses into despondency:

> "I falter where I firmly trod;
> And falling, with my weight of cares,
> Upon the world's great altar-stairs
> That slope through darkness up to God,"—

he feels "the weight of loss is ever there."

It is the final note of the first period, that of "Sorrow unopposed," which closes at Section LV.:

> "O life! as futile, then, as frail!
> O for thy voice to soothe and bless!
> What hope of answer, or redress?—
> Behind the veil; behind the veil."

In the first period, then, we have traversed seven

more or less defined phases or moods of sorrow: first, he is stunned; second, he realizes his loss; third, he awakes to find all outward things are so many endless reflections of his grief; fourth, he turns from the consolation of friends, to intellectual speculation; fifth, thence to prayer; sixth, thence to desponding confession of ignorance; seventh, relapse into hopelessness. He has throughout been the sport of moods which chased each other in rapid succession: *he is overcome without a struggle.*

II. SORROW OPPOSED.—In this period, from LV. to LXXXII., *he struggles, and is overcome.* To all moods, however dismal, belong merciful reactions, and in seasons of deep sorrow we sometimes feel angry because we cannot be always sad: we resent any lifting of the cloud, any approach to levity or laughter. The mood in which recovery is possible begins with a more quiet contemplation —an ability to face the sad aspect of lost love calmly. The friend of the dead lies awake, and sees in imagination the distant moonlight stealing over the memorial tablet of Arthur Hallam, just as it steals over the walls of his own bedchamber.

And now the second Christmas is already upon him, and the months have brought with them a slow and silent change: he cannot but be affected by the inability of the young and happy around him to be ever brooding over past pain; he is shocked, but only half-shocked:

> "Who show'd a token of distress?
> No single tear, no mark of pain!
> O sorrow! then can sorrow wane?
> O grief! can grief be changed to less?"

He seeks for the note of a reconciling term—he finds it:

> "O last regret, regret can die!
> No; mixt with all this mystic frame,
> Her deep relations are the same,
> But with long use her tears are dry."

He is beginning to acquiesce in this shifting of moods, when, with one of those sudden emotional bursts to which sensitive spirits are liable, there comes upon him the vision of what might have been—his friend sitting "crowned with good," married to a beloved sister of the poet, himself an honoured guest, the children babbling "uncle" on his knee; the happy social converse of kindred spirits; "of later genial table-talk, or deep dispute and graceful jest." It was one of those sudden day-dreams, that depart as swiftly, leaving us the more forlorn.

> "What reed was that on which I leant?
> Ah, backward fancy, wherefore wake
> The old bitterness again, and break
> The low beginnings of content?"

Thus the four stages of the second period, in which he struggles and is overcome, are also marked: 1st, more quiet contemplation; leading to, 2nd, more normal acceptance of life, as marked at Christmas-time; 3rd, followed by more resigned views of death; when, 4th, the low beginnings of content are suddenly dissipated by a vision of memory and anticipation, and the first recovering mood is thus baffled.

III. SORROW CONQUERED.—A transition period may be indicated at Stanza LXXXIV.:

> "This truth came borne with bier and pall—
> I felt it, when I sorrow'd most—
> 'Tis better to have loved and lost,
> Than never to have loved at all."

But he will not admit that his love is really less intense:

> "And so my passion hath not swerved
> To works of weakness, but I find
> An image comforting the mind,
> And in my grief a strength reserved."

Sooner or later the sane voices of common day make themselves heard. You have no right to be prostrated in such a manner as not to rise out of sorrow, misfortune, or calamity; it may press you down, but you should struggle out of it, and face life again, with all its great responsibilities; you should return to life a deeper, truer, more many-sided human being, than you were before. By virtue of what you are, you must go back and re-enter the arena of life; the inner voices drive you there, it is your destiny; and as long as a spark of vitality remains, nature reminds you of the inexorable needs of a loving and responsive soul:

> "My heart, tho' widow'd, may not rest
> Quite in the love of what is gone,
> But seeks to beat in time with one
> That warms another living breast."

So, you see, one object after another may be taken away, but the capacity to love does not cease. " Friend after friend departs! Who has not lost a friend?" But your heart will still require some object; the heart must grind something; if you do not give it good corn to grind, it will grind its very self to pieces. God has so ordered and set this world, that objects of affection may, one after another, be taken away, and yet the healthy susceptibilities of the heart have still something left to do; they wake up from the sleep of sorrow, hungry, and thirsty, and eager. If you will only lift up your eyes, there are still men and women willing to be loved, still interests and objects worthy to be pursued. And indeed you have no right to shut yourself up, when there is a whole world crying out for sympathy, when help is so much needed, when there are so many poor forsaken ones, who would give anything for a little of your kindness, and thought, and feeling, which you are consuming on yourself, or on some object which has been taken away from your gaze for ever.

So the poet and teacher speaks aloud to all prostrated by sorrow, failure, disappointment, or loss, of "the mighty hopes which make us men." These it cannot suit him to forget, and his pulses begin to beat again "for other friends that once he met."

Here is struck the true note of the true heart of a man or woman arising out of the depths of despair, and out of the paralysis of grief, to something like a healthy perception of human life again. And above and beyond the voices of affliction, he seems to hear his beloved friend himself saying,—

> "Arise, and get thee forth, and seek
> A friendship for the years to come."

From this time, having indissolubly associated his friend with the change, peace seems to dawn upon his perturbed spirit; and now, instead of being *reflected by* outward nature, he *reflects* it, and bathes himself in the light, and drinks in eagerly the refreshing and invigorating influences of the happy spring:

> "Wild bird, whose warble, liquid sweet,
> Rings Eden thro' the budded quicks,
> O tell me where the senses mix,
> O tell me where the passions meet."

Or—

> "Sweet after showers, ambrosial air,
> That rollest from the gorgeous gloom
> Of evening over brake and bloom."

In this mood of reserved strength, with a restored balance of perception he can go back to the very scenes of his college life. He revisits Trinity

College, passes through the tall avenues, over the bridge, lingers by the river, in the street, in the College hall and chapel—and, strange enough, it is without pain, but in softened lines of happy memory, that he recalls his friend's life and converse in those haunts of undergraduate life. But one cry breaks from him—of passion, more than of despair—when he thinks how many dead, once wept for, are now unmourned :

> " Ah dear, but come thou back to me :
> Whatever change the years have wrought,
> I find not yet one lonely thought
> That cries against my wish for thee."

But we have entered upon the third period, in which he struggles and overcomes. The tone has grown more sober, the poignant grief is passing away, and his sorrow is more like a pathetic memory than a present pain. When the third Christmas comes round, it is not like the first, drowned in tears; nor yet like the second, when the inability to grieve continuously is almost met with impatience; but the bells sound the joyous and triumphant note of the Christmas season. Wider than any individual grief or joy is that message of peace on earth and goodwill towards men.

To him it is the "resurgam" of healthy sensibility and hopefulness; and the strain that now rises is full of victory and praise:

> "Ring out, wild bells, to the wild sky,
>   The flying cloud, the frosty light:
>   The year is dying in the night;
> Ring out, wild bells, and let him die.
>
> Ring out the old, ring in the new;
>   Ring, happy bells, across the snow:
>   The year is going, let him go;
> Ring out the false, ring in the true.
>
> Ring out the grief that saps the mind,
>   For those that here we see no more;
>   Ring out the feud of rich and poor;
> Ring in redress to all mankind.
>
> * * * * *
>
> Ring out old shapes of foul disease;
>   Ring out the narrowing lust of gold;
>   Ring out the thousand wars of old;
> Ring in the thousand years of peace.
>
> Ring in the valiant man and free,
>   The larger heart, the kindlier hand;
>   Ring out the darkness of the land;
> Ring in the Christ that is to be."

IV. PEACE.—That jubilant melody sweet as

the angels' Peace on earth, and goodwill to men, heralds us into the last period of peace. He has now triumphed over sorrow. The dark past rolls away like a cloud, leaving the horizon clear. The bells have rung out the weary load of suffering, and rung in human fellowship, sympathy, and a new content :

> "I will not shut me from my kind;
>   And lest I stiffen into stone,
>   I will not eat my heart alone,
> Nor feed with sighs a passing wind."

And of that new communion, that restored and vigorous life, chastened at the outset by pain and loss, we have reaped the rich harvest, as year after year one noble and representative song after another has rolled forth "from that clear harp in divers tones," enriching, beautifying, and raising the literature of our age to the highest levels of imagination and thought.

The Poets of the age—those who read the inner life of the time, and form it—are ever the measure of its conduct, philosophy, and achievement; and nobly has Tennyson fulfilled his mission.

At the close of the "In Memoriam" outward

nature sinks back into her appointed place, and is seen for the first time in right proportion to the soul; she is no longer the slave of his sensibility, reflecting all his moods, or a tyrant imposing her own. She is no longer seen subjectively, but has become sweetly objective. She is the garden of Eden, in which he walks, which ministers to him, consoles, thrills, soothes, and delights him.

And now, with an intuitive sense of artistic finish and completeness—such as we observe in Mendelssohn, when his opening phrase recurs at the close of some lengthy movement, suggesting what has gone before, and yet changing and completing it in the very suggestion—there comes back the vision of the beloved friend; but his form is changed; his face glows in the distant light of heaven; he looks out upon us as in a vision; he is rapt for ever now from the fickle and the frail—the distance is immeasurable. The friend looks up, and no longer thinks of bridging over the gulph; but he sees beyond it, and his soul grows calm in the softened light, as the last spiritualized vision of his friend passes before him:

> "Dear friend, far off, my lost desire—
> So far, so near in woe and weal;

O loved the most when most I feel
There is a lower and a higher;

Known and unknown; human, divine;
  Sweet human hand, and lips, and eye;
  Dear heavenly friend, that canst not die,—
Mine, mine, for ever; ever mine;

Strange friend—past, present, and to be;
  Loved deeplier, darklier understood;
  Behold, I dream a dream of good,
And mingle all the world with thee."

How different is this from the former strains of wild sorrow, restless doubt, brooding sadness, and despair!

It is this "strange friend," so spiritualized, who leads his own spirit to find that supreme rest in God with which the poem concludes. After the whirlwind, and the storm, and the fire, comes the still small voice. Grief, and agony, and doubt, and all the miserable speculations which haunt and corrode the inner life, have been swept away; the bitter and fragmentary experiences have at last "orbed into a perfect whole." The entire period of probation stands out, and the human heart owns the accomplished work. And thus, through love possessed and lost, the soul has been lifted into that heavenly sphere in which life grows sweet and wholesome once more, and all love is found again in God.

> "Now fades the last long streak of snow;
>   Now burgeons every maze of quick
>   About the flowering squares, and thick
> By ashen roots the violets blow.
>
> Now rings the woodland loud and long,
>   The distance takes a lovelier hue,
>   And drown'd in yonder living blue
> The lark becomes a sightless song."

In this period of peace we get those large and mellowed utterances which raise the poem above all transitory or accidental circumstances, and give it that peculiar glow of radiant and supernal beauty:

> "That which we dare invoke to bless;
>   Our dearest faith; our ghastliest doubt:
>   He, they, one, all; within, without;
> The power in darkness whom we guess;
>
> I found him not in world or sun,
>   Or eagle's wing, or insect's eye;
>   Nor thro' the questions men may try,
> The petty cobwebs we have spun:
>
> If e'er, when faith had fall'n asleep,
>   I heard a voice 'Believe no more,'
>   And heard an ever breaking shore
> That tumbled in the Godless deep;

A warmth within the breast would melt
   The freezing reason's colder part,
   And, like a man in wrath, the heart
Stood up and answer'd 'I have felt.'

No, like a child in doubt and fear:
   But that blind clamour made me wise;
   Then was I as a child that cries,
But crying knows his father near;

And what I seem beheld again
   What is, and no man understands;
   And out of darkness came the hands
That reach thro' nature, moulding men."

And what remains of broken tendrils, unsolved mysteries, unsatisfied longings, are also brought together at last, and left in the Divine keeping—"in manus tuas, Domine!"

"O living Will! that shall endure
   When all that seems shall suffer shock!
   Rise in the spiritual rock;
Flow thro' our deeds and make them pure,

That we may lift from out the dust
   A voice as unto Him that hears,—
   A cry above the conquer'd years
To One that with us works; and trust,

With faith that comes of self-control,
   The truths that never can be proved
   Until we close with all we loved,
And all we flow from, soul in soul."

V.

Robert Browning.

NEW YEAR'S EVE.

V.

Robert Browning.

NEW YEAR'S EVE.

THIS evening's meditation does not pretend to give an estimate of Robert Browning's works. Critically, therefore, it is narrowed into this: a study in Robert Browning for the purposes of edification and devout thought. I shall deal mainly with a poem entitled "Christmas Eve and Easter Day," stopping short of the Easter Day portion—in reality a separate poem.

Like the wise man of old, the wise men of this and every other age ask "Who are our true spiritual teachers?" We are all looking for stars in the East. From the Milky Way—from the tangled nebulæ—from the transient fires that flash and pass—these Eastern lights slowly but surely disengage themselves, and orb into solitary splendour as each century waxes and wanes.

The first ten years of a man's life-work seldom fixes his position, although the work then done sometimes does. Not all who dazzle are destined to reign; not all who reign, are at first seen to wear the imperial purple. Now that the century grows old, we can see who have been its teachers in religion, science, art, painting, poetry; and Tennyson and Browning are probably the two names which will be chosen to follow the great Lake School of Wordsworth; just as Schumann and Wagner are the two real representatives of German music, after Beethoven.

Time decides slowly, but inexorably; in the long run, the "vox populi" is the "vox Dei;" its judgment is not capricious, but exact, logical, axiomatic.

How the great names that win have been at first derided or ignored, is a painful and instructive commonplace. Some of us can remember the time when John Henry Newman was accounted a mere sectarian fanatic, with a weakness for Popery and prelacy; when Frederick Maurice was dismissed as an amiable mystic with a taint of heresy; when Herbert Spencer and John Stuart Mill were simply not read. I can recollect the mixed rage and pleasantry which greeted Mr. Ruskin's "Stones of Venice" and the "Seven Lamps of Architecture"— the storm of ridicule which threatened to blight Pre-

Raphaelism in art—the pitying smile with which one's elders greeted the rising appreciation of Tennyson, whom Bulwer, that splendid literary Philistine, called "Miss Alfred." Jests about the Music of the Future, and Wagner, are only just beginning to sound old and out of place. And we may recall how, a few years ago, the gifted Elizabeth Barrett Browning, now almost forgotten, was thought a greater poet than her husband—just as Byron was preferred to Wordsworth, and Moore to Shelley.

I. BROWNING'S CHARACTERISTICS.—What has given Browning his peculiar and increasing hold over our age? As a singer he has been surpassed by many inferior men. I had almost said he seldom sings. But he is a poet for all that, and he can sing, and sing sweetly too when he pleases. But he is chiefly dear to the age as a feeler and a thinker; he is also dear because knowing all, and having been racked with its doubts, and stretched upon the mental torture-wheels of his time, he does not despair. Having sounded cynicism and pessimism to their depths, he comes by a very different road to the same crowning conclusion as his brother poets, Tennyson and Longfellow; and sometimes firmly, and sometimes faintly, trusts the larger hope, but always in the last analysis and residuum of thought—trusts. Coming from such a mind—such a buoyant message this vexed and storm-tossed age will not willingly let die. It clings to Browning; it bears with his moods; it even buys much that it cannot understand, and more that it does not attempt to read; it lays "Paracelsus" aside; it confesses never to have quite got through that work as unique and as representative of our age as the "In Memoriam" —I allude to "The Ring and the Book." But Browning must be in the house.

Browning is our friend; we take him by the hand; we feel we can trust him; he is equally incapable of lying or cajolery. We say to him, you have the brain of juggler; you have the insight and sensibility of the poet, the soul of an artist; you pretend to look on, and analyze, and describe, sometimes coldly, even cynically; but you care not if we see the honest generous face through the thin mask; for in reality you *agonize* over all you do; you know all and see all; nothing eludes the vigilance of your incisive intellect; and what lies beyond its reach is brought fluttering to your feet by flashes of surprizing intuition. And the faculty for which we prize you most is just this, that you have an inexhaustible interest in human nature; that you love "man and woman;" that you believe in the soul and in God.

It was not easy for the public to find all this out at first. Browning had no Gospel to plead, no theory or plan of life to announce. What he was, what he could teach, came to us, probably as it came to him, spontaneously and by degrees. As the French say, he allowed himself to be divined. Never was Stuart Mill's definition of poetry more happily and vigorously illustrated than in Browning's poems: " Poetry is the expression of thought coloured by emotion, expressed in metre, and *overheard.*"

It is what we overhear as he thinks out loud which rivets, and wraps our senses nearer to the poet's inmost soul.

Browning's obscurity, and occasional incapacity to express himself simply, is often compensated by a direct and astonishing vigour of expression, which strikes home with the force of a sledge hammer.

"Fear death?—to feel the fog in my throat,
   The mist in my face,

When the snows begin, and the blasts denote
  I am nearing the place,
The power of the night, the press of the storm,
  The host of the foe,
Where He stands the Arch Fear, in a visible form?
  Yet the strong man must go."

With characteristic boldness he faces the crisis—leaps across the very chasm of death, into the life beyond :

" I was ever a fighter ; so one fight more,
  The best and the last !
I would hate that death bandaged my eyes and forbore,
  And bade me creep past.
No ! let me taste the whole of it fair, like my peers
  The heroes of old ;
Bear the brunt ; in a minute pay glad life's arrears
  Of pain, darkness, and cold.
For sudden the worst turns the best to the brave ;
  The black minute's at end ;
And the elements' rage, the fiends' voices' rave,
  Shall dwindle and blend—
Shall change—shall become, first a peace, then a joy—
  Then a light.   *   *   *

I recall but one other instance in which the dread passage of the soul has been described in poetry; and it is curious to contrast the terrible realism of Browning, with Pope's splendid burst of artificial eloquence in " The Dying Christian to his Soul :"

> " Vital spark of heavenly flame,
> Quit, oh quit this mortal frame !
> Trembling, hoping, ling'ring, flying—
> Oh the pain, the bliss, of dying !
> Cease, fond nature, cease thy strife,
> And let me languish into life.
>
> Hark ! they whisper ! Angels say,
> ' Sister spirit, come away :'
> What is this absorbs me quite,
> Steals my senses, shuts my sight,
> Drowns my spirit, draws my breath—
> Tell me, my soul, can this be death?
>
> The world recedes—it disappears ;
> Heaven opens on my eyes; my ears
>   With sounds seraphic ring !
> Lend, lend, your wings. I mount ! I fly !
> O grave, where is thy victory ?
>   O death, where is thy sting ?

But not only for the sake of his force, but also for his subtlety, the student of Browning is patient with his obscurity; and often his very failure to express simply, gives him strange power to express what others could not render at all. He revels in the abstruse and difficult, like a consummate executive musician, who bungles over a simple tune and glories in almost impossible difficulties. "Caliban upon Setebos" is an example. The dull gropings after the natural religion of terror by a being half brute half human—the instinctive analysis of the world, untouched by the glow of an awakened spirit in man and unillumined by the love of God,—the speculation and sentiment in "Caliban upon Setebos" is, in short, the whole argument needful to enforce the necessity of a Divine sustained communication between God and man. It images graphically what the life of man—what his feeling towards the unseen would have been, had there been no inner teaching, no development of religion, no Divine intercommunion. The human nature in Caliban shuts up all those elements in us which cry out for a living and a loving God—a God manifest in the flesh.

There was never a poet at once so graphic—so capable of painting with a few spots of colour, and yet so independent of what is graphic and external. Caliban is full of an eastern glow of colour—a minute detail and observation of external nature, worthy of a naturalist; but the whole is nothing but a mental drama, played out on the lowest level of human intelligence—as "Luria" is a drama played out on the highest. All Browning's poems are nothing but "dramas of the inner life." He cares really for nothing but metaphysics. Religion, philosophy, science, art, help him to this; but all save the unseen motives which pass "hither and thither dividing the swift mind," is framework—machinery; or so much paint, which might be rubbed off, and still leave the contour of his work perfect. His power lies wholly in atmosphere. The scene is chosen for the atmosphere—the atmosphere is never chosen for the scene; the plot is for the emotion—never the emotion for the plot. But throughout one great moral quality emerges—one of which no age ever tires, of which no age ever stood in such sore need as ours—the passionate love of truth rather than repose. "God," says Emerson, "offers to every man truth and repose; between these two, man as a pendulum ever oscillates." Browning never. Through all its contradictory windings he will know and have the very heart in man and woman. He is a great unveiler; he tears off the mask, tramples the sham underfoot, shows people to themselves and to the world, weighs them in the balance, tries them in the crucible, sets the pure gold in his heart of hearts, and flings the dross passionately to the four winds of heaven. For him no rounded whole, no sham consistency, at the expense of truth. Let us all stand fair, and be judged with all our imperfections on our heads—" nothing extenuate, nor set down aught in malice." In Browning the unattainable is never attained—the ideal is never reached : there is never a perfect saint or villain throughout the whole of his works. Yet is he no pessimist—no real cynic; for the sense of Divine perfection is also never lost; it is the deep undertone of life, amidst its wildest discords. He is passionately wedded to this world; everything about it is full of teeming interest for him; and yet the motto he has selected for death rules life —it is the eternal " Prospice " or " Beyond ! "

Thus much must suffice for " characteristics."

II. THE DISSENTING CHAPEL.—I pass to Browning the truth-seeker, sifter of sects and ceremonies. In the singular poem called " Christmas-Eve," we have three impersonated atmospheres—independent religion, conventional religion, spiritual religion ; or the power of the poem may be better marshalled as the Truth-Seeker between the religion of the sects and the spirit of Christ. The situations are universal and recurrent. We, too, have stood in church, and chapel, and lecture-room, and looked on. We, too, have had glimpses of the Christ that comprehends the churches, and whom the churches cannot comprehend.

A thin dream-veil of intense drama, like a heated film of human passion, is thrown over this narrative of a soul in travail. Its homely and familiar flashes draw us only nearer to the poet's thought; for have not our souls too been in travail? Have not we stood and listened in little chapels, and sat in dismal churches, and lingered in cathedral aisles, and watched the light through jewelled panes, and heard the mellowed organ-thunder roll?

> "Out of the little chapel I burst,
> Into the fresh night-air again."

What brought him there: wind and rain, on the verge of a lonely common; and something besides, perchance? About all universal experiences there is a spell, which no one quite shakes off: about death, as we turn to look at a funeral; an accident in the street we crowd to

K

see; happy children we follow with wistful eyes; a regiment of soldiers, representing corporate effort and heroism,—all large crowds attract and fascinate. Religious gatherings always possess this potent spell. Whoever stood in a church porch without peeping inside, especially if the church was crowded? The "Seeker" enters "Sion Chapel"—a motley gathering of the poorer sort, but all well schooled in the Baptist, or Calvinist, or Wesleyan 'ism, and resolved to know no other:

> "'What you, the alien, you have ventured
> To take with us, the elect, your station,
> Who cares for none of it—a Gallio!'
> Thus, plain as a print, I read the glance."

The first note of the inner drama is now sounded in the internal protest,—

> "Good folks!
> This way you perform the Grand Inquisitor;
> You are the men, and wisdom shall die with you!
> * * * * *
> Still, as I say, though you've found salvation,
> If I should choose, and now, to cry 'Shares,'
> * * * * *
> Mine's the same right with your poorest and sickliest!"

The Seeker then in no measured terms declares,—

> "I very soon had enough of it—
> The hot smell, and the human noises,
> And the lead-like pressure
> Of the preaching-man's immense stupidity!"

Alas! alas! that intelligent and not ill-disposed men should ever be able to come to church, as well as to chapel, and to go out thinking, if not saying, much the same thing!

> "There was a lull in the rain—a lull
> In the wind too; the moon was risen."

As he walks on, his thoughts come crowding fast and thick, in diffuse meditation:

> "The sermon now—what a mingled weft
> Of good and ill;   *   *   *
> The zeal was good, and the aspiration.
>   *   *   *   *   *
> These people have really felt, no doubt,
> A something—the motion they style the 'call' of them."

And then they seek for the

> "Bringing about
>   *   *   *   *   *
> A sort of reviving and reproducing,
> More or less perfectly (who can tell?),
> Of the mood itself."

But now notice that the contemplation of other worship, however distasteful, forces him inward, to sound his own religion. Place yourself in the current; forsake not the assembling of yourselves together; let the tide of human instincts reach,—it will teach you to know yourself. Can you say with the Seeker, when differing, or repelled, from other forms of faith,—

> "I have my own church.
> * * * * *
> In youth I look'd to these very skies,
> And probing their immensities
> I found God there, His visible power
> Yet felt in my heart; amid all its sense
> Of the power, an equal evidence
> That His love, there too, was the nobler dower?"

And then follows a passage, which, to my mind, points to the central ground of our belief that all is well—that, in a life beyond, the broken lights will come together, the discords find their concord.

Browning has never soared higher than in this new argument from analogy, that as the small intelligence of man conceives the fitting and needful and right, the large intelligence, manifested in Creation, cannot fall short of man's measure,—nay, must realize and transcend it. It is the thought expressed by Sidgwick, our latest moral philosopher, in his profound book "Methods of Ethics"

—that our reason revolts from a world so irrationally constituted, that a course of conduct which is best for the community should ultimately be found a failure for the individual—which moral conduct would occasionally seem to be, if there be no life beyond.

Listen now to the Poet Seeker's faith, as reasonable as it is consolatory and sublime! I wish I could quote it entire. How often do we ask, "Aye! but how do I know that God is good? that I shall live and be satisfied by-and-by? that love which never found its earthly close shall there see of the travail of its soul and be satisfied? And the answer comes:

" All is God's!

*   *   *   *   *

So, gazing up in my youth at love
As seen through power, ever above
All modes which make it manifest,
My soul brought all to a single test—
That He, the Eternal First and Last,
Who in His power had so surpass'd
All man conceives of what is might—
Whose wisdom, too, show'd infinite—
Would prove as infinitely good;
Would never (my soul understood),
With power to work all love desires,

Bestow e'en less than man requires—
That He who endlessly was teaching,
Above my spirit's utmost reaching,
What love can do in the leaf or stone,
Would never need that I, in turn,
Should point Him out defect unheeded,
And show that God had yet to learn
What the meanest human creature needed—
Not life, to wit, for a few short years
Tracking his way through doubts and fears.

* * * * *

No ; love, which on earth, amid all the shows of it,
Has ever been seen the sole food of life in it—
The love ever growing there, spite of the strife in it,
Shall arise made perfect, from Death's repose of it.
And I shall behold Thee face to face,
O God, and in Thy light retrace
How in all I loved here still wast Thou !
Whom pressing to, then, as I fain would now,
I shall find as able to satiate
The love, Thy gift, as my spirit's wonder
Thou art able to quicken and sublimate
With this sky of Thine that I now walk under,
And glory in Thee for, as I gaze—
Thus ! thus ! Oh, let men keep their ways
Of seeking Thee in a narrow shrine ;
Be this my way ! And this is mine !"

II. THE DIVINE APPARITION.—Is he in the little chapel, or out of it ? He seems to be outside, on the lonely moorland, at night. But the place matters not; he is in the spirit. The dream, the trance, the ecstasy is all. He looks up—

> "The rain and the wind ceased, and the sky
>   Received at once the full fruition
>   Of the moon's consummate apparition."

In that moment his soul, at its highest tension, is very near to God. The skies bend down to him; he is aware of a power and presence, and his open vision begins, his whole frame quivering with intense excitement.

> "All at once I looked up with terror:
> *He* was there   *   *   *
> He Himself, with his human hair,
> On the narrow pathway, just before:
> I saw the back of Him—no more.
> He had left the chapel then, as I.
> I forgot all about the sky.
> No face: only the sight
> Of a sweeping garment, vast and white,
> With a hem that I could recognize.
> I felt no terror—no surprise.
> My mind filled with the cataract
> At one bound of the mighty fact!
> I remember He did say,
> Doubtless, that, to the world's end,
> Where two or three should meet and pray
> He would be in their midst—their Friend.
> Certainly He was there with them!"

The Lord Christ makes as though He would pass on, but—

> "I hasten'd—cried out, while I press'd
> To the salvation of the Vest—
> 'But not so, Lord! It cannot be
> That Thou indeed art leaving me—
> Me, that have despised Thy friends
> Did my heart make no amends?
> Thou art the love of God!'"

And suddenly, as he pours forth his wild supplication, his—

> "Body is caught up in the whirl and drift
> Of the Vesture's amplitude, still eddying
> On, just before."

His own heart, with true love trembling, no more scorning the Lord's friends in the little chapel, is accepted by the Lord and Master of both.

III. IN ST. PETER'S AT ROME.—In a moment the scene changes: we are at Rome; the mighty basilica of St. Peter—

> "Is alive.
> Men in the chancel, body, and nave—
> Men on the pillar and architrave—
> Men on the statues—men on the tombs;
> All famishing in expectation
> Of the main-altar consummation."

It is the Popish mass—the doctrine, the superstition, of transubstantiation. And Christ enters: Christ enters the Roman church as well as the dissenting chapel; and he, the Seeker, repelled by Romish superstition, as he has been by Protestant ignorance and vulgarity—he, the Seeker, is again left without :

"'Yes,' I said, 'that He will go
And sit with these in turn, I know.
Their faith's heart beats, though her head swims
Too giddily to guide her limbs.
* * * * *
* * Though Rome's gross robe
Drops off, no more to be endured,
Her teaching is not so obscured
By errors and perversities,
That no truth shines athwart the bier.
And He whose eye detects a spark,
Even where to man's the whole seems dark,
May well see flame."

In another moment he is in the great basilica, and his voice swells the strain of common praise:

"I see the error; but above
The scope of error, see the love!"

As between sect and sect, church and chapel, Romanist and Protestant, his lesson has been learned :

> "I will be wise another time,
> And not desire a wall between us
> When next I see a church-roof cover
> So many species of one genus,
> All with their foreheads bearing Lover
> Written above the earnest eyes of them."

IV. THE GERMAN LECTURE-ROOM.—Once more his body is—

> "Caught up in the whirl and drift
> Of the Vesture's amplitude, still eddying
> On, just before him."

Is he not now worthy to enter everywhere? Twice in despising the intellectual narrowness and bigotry of others, he has been convicted of a cold and narrow heart himself. Surely now he may enter everywhere. But no; he is once more outside—outside a sort of temple, perhaps a college, somewhere in Germany—at Tubingen or Göttingen. It is probably Dr. Strauss, the great destructive German critic, who is lecturing inside—lecturing with intense earnestness, no doubt, and lecturing on Christ too. And Christ enters! whilst the Truth Seeker enters not, but just looks in, and sees the Professor facing his rows of attentive pupils, a martyr to mild enthusiasm. The discourse is destructive of much of the framework of the Gospel history, but it is earnest, high toned, and moral; and there is something even in that throng of attentive students which attracts the Christ; but the Seeker on the threshold thus sums up his three experiences of Dissenters, Papists, and Critic :

> "This time He would not bid me enter
> The exhausted air-bell of the critic.
> Truth's atmosphere may grow mephitic
> When Papist struggles with Dissenter.
> * * * * *
> Each that thus sets the pure air seething
> May poison it for healthy breathing.
> But the Critic leaves no air to poison—
> Pumps out, with ruthless ingenuity,
> Atom by atom, and leaves you—vacuity."

It is not likely that Mr. Browning would at this time of day speak of the results of German criticism in these inadequate terms. We must remember that this satire on Strauss was written in 1849, when people in England were so terrified at the destructive critics abroad, that they failed to see the extent to which the new research and learning was preparing a new mould for the Christian idea. In fact, we have gained enormously by all this minute and honest examination of the Old and New Testaments. We really gather for the first time what the life of Christ and His disciples must, in the main situations, have been; what the people were—the Romans, the Jews, the Greeks; what Rome, and Jerusalem, and the Mediterranean Isles, and the fair provinces of Asia Minor, with their Greek settlements, and little Jewries dotted about in every important town—what, in fine, the world was under Tiberius Cæsar and Nero. We see now how the Gospels came together; we separate between those elements derived from the apostles at Jerusalem, the little group of friends who clung to our Lord's family in exile, and the free Pauline element, which failed to mould the Christianity of the two first centuries, but has dominated the remaining sixteen hundred years of the Christian era.

The Truth Seeker of 1849 would not see, what is evident now, how that many of his difficulties of belief would be solved, not by any fresh attempt to swallow obsolete dogmas called distinctively Christian, but by such a re-statement of Bible inspiration, the divinity of Christ, the future life of man, the Divine Presence with him here, as would make these truths as tenable and self-evident in their new form as they were tenable and self-evident in the old forms which we are still struggling to be free of. And how helpful the new criticism was going to be to the reconstruction of theology, Mr. Browning could not possibly then see; but we see, it, and rejoice in it. Still, with a fine instinct, the poet notes that Christ enters the critic's lecture-room, although he is excluded. He seems then to grow a little uneasy at his own strictures :

> "Could my soul find aught to sing in tune with,
> Even at this lecture, if she tried ? "

And further on, remembering his mistaken scorn of Sion chapel :

> "Unlearned love was safe from spurning ;
> Can't we respect your loveless learning ?"

Which he could not, for he did not really understand its drift. He could only sneer at the Professor recommending us to go on looking up to Christ, after robbing Him of His divinity. For the first time the Seeker becomes something like a cynic. He is now convinced of every one's imbecility as regards religious matters, and he is willing that every one should call themselves Christian, or anything they please, as long as they let him alone with his own pet beliefs. The communion with loving souls which he was beginning to find whilst keeping close to Christ, is thus abruptly broken. But with the entrance in of this cynical indifference—with this loss of love—Christ has also departed.

The calm of the night has passed—the horrible storm begun afresh : " Because thou art neither hot nor cold, therefore I will spew thee out of My mouth ! "

Indifference is, after all, the one thing which separates from Christ—which damns:

> "The black night caught me in his mesh,
> Whirl'd me up, and flung me prone ;
> I look'd, and far there, ever fleeting—
> Far, far away—the receding gesture,
> And looming of the lessening Vesture,
> Swept forward from my stupid hand,
> While I watch'd my foolish heart expand,
> In the lazy glow of benevolence,
> O'er the various modes of man's belief."

Roused by the fear of losing his Divine Guide—

> " I caught at the flying robe unrepell'd,
> Was lapp'd again in its folds, full fraught
> With warmth, and wonder, and delight,
> God's mercy being infinite !
> For scarce had the words escaped my tongue,
> When, at a passionate bound, I sprung
> Out of the wandering world of rain,
> Into the little chapel again."

The dream—for it was a dream—is over. The soul had its troubled starting from a poor little dissenting chapel; it had gone a pilgrimage thence with its Lord; it had learnt at last that separation from man was separation from God— that they who best commune with Him can best commune in love with each other. Before men's frailties and bigotries, scorn is out of place, for the best of us are frail and narrow compared with Him; before the religion of the heart, learning and intellect stand abashed; that is a holy of holies, open to the poorest and meanest, into which they enter not; they may become its sentinels and outside ministers—it can never become theirs. The incense of prayer shall rise for ever and ever from a thousand temples and ten thousand tongues, but the essence and core of religion is one and indivisible, in all ages and in all climes; it is the discovery of love, the appropriation of love, the offering of love—often revealed to babes, and sometimes hidden from the wise and learned.

"He prayeth best who loveth best."

VI.

Keble.

THE "HIGH CHURCH" AND THE CHRISTIAN YEAR.

VI.

Keble.

THE "HIGH CHURCH" AND THE CHRISTIAN YEAR.

N discussing Keble and "The Christian Year," I shall not merely read a few extracts and make a few comments, but I shall try to give you a clear view, if only in outline, of the great High Church movement, in its first, as well as in that second development in the midst of which we are now living.

There is nothing so improving to the mind as to hold together the great religious movements of each age, in their right connexion. They are none of them isolated phenomena, the eccentricities of priests or people. They have their origin, rise, progress, and decay. You can never do them, or the men that lead them, justice until you understand *that*. You must note how one movement of thought, one set of men, one class of books, come from certain states, tendencies, and necessities of the age. And therefore it is instructive and desirable to trace how the High Church, the Low Church, and the Broad Church movements came about. I shall leave the Broad Church movement alone to-night, and proceed to trace Ritualism to its source.

I. THE EVANGELICAL MOVEMENT. — The old Evangelical movement in the early part of the present century was still living on the impulse of Wesley, in the persons of Newton, Romaine, and Dr. Haweis, rector of Aldwinckle, first chaplain to the Countess of Huntingdon, and her executor.

But the real life of religion had run, or was daily being successfully forced by the old dry-church party, into dissenting channels. Robert Hall, Jay of Bath, and others, had passed away, leaving imitators, such as McNeile of Liverpool, Melville, and Close, who expressed powerfully enough the expiring force of the movement intellectually, and Edward Irving, who seemed, previous to his fanatical outburst, destined to re-clothe its threadbare theology.

The strength of the old Evangelical movement was the depth of its personal religion; and the weakness of it was its anarchy, its religious lawlessness,

its want of culture, and its narrow fanaticism. But
what the Evangelical, or Low Church movement,
did for England, was to restore the spiritual element
to the life of the everyday world, just as their suc-
cessors of the High Church restored the spiritual
element to the services of the church; but the
Low Church did its work by trampling upon
forms and ceremonies—the High Church by exalting them, as we shall presently see. Still the
Evangelicals made men look within; they roused
the conscience; they preached the terrors of the
Lord, the doctrine of conversion and sweet inward
peace in Jesus. They stood for the conscious
communion between the soul and God, independent of, though not unassisted by, sacraments, but
hardly independent of rousing pulpit eloquence.
Their activity and earnestness became a flame in
Whitfield, and an organization in Wesley. And
the vitality of the system, like that of so many
other strong constitutions, has long outlived its
intellect, and even its common sense.

In 1839, on the centenary of Methodism, a sum
of 216,000*l.* was collected for the objects of the
society; in 1851 there were 428 circuits, with

between 13,000 and 14,000 local preachers, about 920 itinerant preachers; and now there are considerably more than 6580 chapels. Well, all this energy ought to have been taken up by the church; and if our bishops and clergy had known what they were about with the people when those persons came to stand up and teach, the maternal church should have managed to find room *within* her for this mass of devotional enthusiasts, instead of slamming the door in their faces. It is a scandal, and a reflection upon Church of England policy and administration, that my grandfather, Dr. Haweis, holding Evangelical opinions, should have died an English rector, whilst a few years later the Lady Huntingdon sect, professing opinions identical with his, should have been thrust out of the Church of England. The church thus lost Joseph Sortain, of Brighton, one of the most refined and eloquent preachers of his day. And I make bold to say, standing in a Church of England pulpit, and being myself a minister of the Established Church, that if it had not been for the religious life expressed now in various forms of dissent, and expressed at the beginning of this century in the shape of the burning Evangelical movement, there would not have been much religion left in this country.

II. THE HIGH CHURCH MOVEMENT.—For the High Church movement we must go back at least to the year 1830; and before we can hope to understand the intellectual or religious aspect of the movement, we must realize the political atmosphere of France and England at this time.

In 1830 the Revolution broke out in Paris: it was the cumulative rebound from the iron despotism of Napoleon. Miserable as it was, it was still the gasping of new-born freedom, so soon to be stifled by the dulness of Louis Philippe and the crimes of Louis Napoleon. In the midst of military conscription and social slavery the people sought the air of freedom—in literature, in art, in politics, and broke out wherever they could into lawlessness and anarchy.

That impulse reached our own shores, but with a certain spent force. Still it set up a profound agitation and political turmoil between the years 1838 and 1847. In 1828 the repeal of the Test and Corporation Acts opened Parliament to dissenters; in 1829 came "Catholic emancipation;" in

1831 Lord John Russell's famous Reform Bill was fought for and won; old institutions were daily threatened; the prelates felt their position in the Lords insecure; the abolition of church-rates was vehemently demanded, by people who thought that the National Church of England had sunk so low that it had better be swept away altogether; the separation of church and state was openly advocated by eloquent writers; and party feeling ran so high that several of the Irish clergy were assassinated in 1834, and ten Irish bishoprics were abolished.

What did all this mean? It meant that in a stirring irritable age the Church of England had lost power with the people. She had lost it mainly by banishing a rash and, it must be said, irritable and somewhat lawless section of the Evangelicals, who were at the close of the last century the life-blood of religion; while those who remained in the church were allowed to do so because they had lost the early glow, and the inconvenient fervour and piety, which characterized the church of Wesley, Romaine, and Haweis of Aldwinckle.

About this time (1830) there came up to Oxford

University a small band of earnest men, deeply evangelical in piety, who mourned over the fact that evangelical religion had sunk so low and had assumed without the pale of the National Church forms so lawless and extravagant. These men sighed for discipline; they sought to revive church order. And what were their names? John Keble; John Henry Newman, now living, and in his 80th year (1880); then Pusey, now Dr. Pusey, in his 80th year; Manning, now Cardinal Manning, in his 68th year; Faber, afterwards Father Faber, the author of the beautiful hymn "The Pilgrims of the Night," &c.; then Mr. Froude; and Mr. Gladstone, the future premier of England; then Palmer, Neale, Percival, and William Gresley, who was for some years identified with the services at St. Paul's, Brighton, whom I had the privilege of knowing, and under whom I had the privilege of sitting in my boyhood.

All these men presented to their fellow-students the aspect of Evangelicals, but added to the characteristic of personal piety, a passionate desire and resolution to restore the church to pristine order and discipline. At this time there was no idea that the movement, if such it could be called, savoured of Rome or Popery. These men were deeply convinced that if the Church of England were to be revived they must take their stand on reverence for the clegry and devotion to the Prayer Book, with a determination to make the utmost, if not the best, possible use of it. But indeed there was much to mend in the current church services, which many of us are old enough to remember. What a dismal affair that "old style" was! the parson in one box and the clerk in another, the parson nodding when the clerk was awake, and the clerk nodding when the parson was awake, and the congregation never awake at all, but dotted about in their high pews dozing through the ceremony, while half-a-dozen professional ladies and gentlemen in a gallery sang or did not sing, as it pleased them, but lolled about, fanning themselves, yawning or whispering, and generally showing the greatest contempt for the whole proceedings.

A peep in imagination only into one of those dry church establishments is quite enough to make us understand the reason why disestablishment and the abolition of church-rates were threatened. At first a simple statement of common aims and objects was agreed upon by the young undergraduates, who met constantly in each other's rooms at Oxford. It was thus worded:

"OBJECTS OF THE ASSOCIATION.

"(1) To maintain pure and inviolate the doctrines, the services, and the discipline of the church; that is, to withstand all changes which involve denial or suppression of doctrine, a departure from primitive practice in religious offices or innovation upon the apostolical prerogatives, order, and communion of bishops, priests, and deacons.

"(2) To afford churchmen an opportunity of exchanging their sentiments, and co-operating together on a large scale."

This they all signed. The suppression of the ten Irish bishoprics called forth Keble's famous sermon on the Great Apostasy; and the Association procured the signatures of 7000 clergymen to a document of a comparatively mild and general character, addressed to the Archbishop of Canterbury, and expressing devotion to "the apostolical order and doctrine of the church," attachment to the "venerable liturgy," "devotion to the orthodox and primitive faith," and a desire "to promote the purity, efficiency, and unity of the church." This seemed at first innocent enough.

In 1834 no less than 23,000 of the laity signed a document in a similar sense, deprecating any separation between church and state, and regreting the latitudinarianism abroad; for another spirit *was* abroad, the infant, though Herculean, throes of the Broad Church. Isaac Taylor had dissected the roots of religious feeling in the " Natural History of Enthusiasm;" Arnold, afterwards Master of Rugby, had advocated a church broad enough to contain dissenters of almost every grade; whilst Maurice, afterwards Professor of Moral Philosophy at Cambridge, who in his later years honoured me with his friendship and counsel, had already, in the "Kingdom of Christ," laid the spiritual foundation of the Church of the Future, in his vivid perception and proclamation of the universal Fatherhood of God.

All this, which seemed to the rising school of earnest devotees of authority and the venerable past, most loose and dangerous doctrine, was, along with the internal apathy of the Establishment, duly denounced by the "Association," lay and clerical. These protests seemed to meet with general public approval—no one was committed to action, and England, startled for a moment at the notion of the church's overthrow, accepted what was in effect the note of revolution as the sign of returning peace and security. But the fact is we are not a revolutionary people ; and if we have our periods of agitation and reform, we are rather frightened afterwards for fear we should have gone too fast and too far. We see this every day in politics, and the consequence is we invariably have a Conservative reaction after a little move forwards. In proof of it, witness the late career of that great statesman, that eloquent political orator, Mr. Gladstone. Having risen to the highest pitch of popularity—having wielded an almost despotic power for a few years—he was suddenly driven from office by a strong Conservative reaction, and the country installed a Conservative statesman at the helm, and sent Lord Beaconsfield to Berlin in 1878.

Following the agitation of 1830, the Evangelical protest signed by 7000 clergymen, and the manifesto signed by 23,000 of the laity, were both warmly received as a general conservative expression of feeling. The old, familiar, all-potent watchwords, Church and State, seemed for a moment to be as powerful to conjure with as ever. The British Constitution must be upheld! Good; but is this what the Oxford movement really meant? Not a bit of it. What did the Newman, Pusey, Manning, and Gladstone of the period really mean? They were quite straightforward, unsuspicious themselves of the inexorable logic of tendency. They meant to restore the church of the first three centuries. Where must they go for information, but to the Church of Rome—Rome the mother of churches? Held she not the keys of all the creeds? the traditions of the elders? the ecclesiastical oracles? So first they learnt what had been done and taught in the first three centuries; they mastered the theology of the fathers, then of the schoolmen, and there they found a good deal which was not done or taught in the primitive church, but as it seemed good and edifying, and generally rousing, they worked it up into their reformed church system, finding the externals of mediæval worship and the internals of ascetic discipline both attractive and fruitful.

This "growth" on the primitive church was covered and accounted for by Newman's Theory of Development, from which it appeared that many things not originally known were the legitimate tendencies of a growing Church. So were slid in a taste for purgatory and the confessional, worship of saints, and prayers for the dead, and under the formal doctrine of apostolical succession, a great deal of sympathy with the supremacy of the Pope as the real head on earth of Christendom.

As regards the Protestant tendencies of the Prayer Book, and the signature of the formularies generally, these were smoothed down by the teaching in Tract 90 (Newman), which held it lawful to sign in a non-natural sense when the natural sense was inconvenient—a happy privilege, which all parties in the church continued to stretch to the utmost, until it broke under the strain, and resulted in the relaxed conditions imposed on the clergy of the Church of England.

Up to the appearance of Tract 90, and indeed for some time after, there seems to have been no intention to aid the cause of Romanism in England. Mr. Palmer, a leading member of the Oxford movement, says, " There was no dishonesty on our part, no wish to promote Romanism, no disloyalty to the Church of England. I might refer (as a proof that the Oxford movement did not mean Rome) to the works of Hook, Gresley, Gladstone, Manning, and very many others;" and later he quotes Pusey against Rome, and dwells with special complacency upon Mr. Newman, as one of those who had said the hardest things against Rome and Romish tendencies. But at that very moment the strongest souls were being borne most swiftly into the bosom of the great mother of churches.

In 1845 Newman, who had created the Tractarian theory, forsook it, and went over to Rome. In 1851 Manning followed his example; and Pusey was freely accused of staying in the English Church in order to make converts for Rome. But to his honour it must be admitted, that a long and faithful life has proved that it was an illogical head, and not a false heart, that prevented Dr. Pusey from seeing the conclusion to his premises. Newman saw that bad was the best that could be said for the Tractarians, and Monsignor Capel has had to explain the same thing to Canon Liddon. Indeed nothing is more unedifying and surprising to the outside public than the ease with which

Roman theologians can disperse the foundations of the Tractarian movement, whenever it pleases some over-zealous ritualist to reconstruct the famous card castle, first built, and then deliberately destroyed, by their greatest champion, and certainly their only thinker.

But I have a little anticipated the course of events. The Tractarian movement made little progress until its friendship for the Pope and its hatred of the English Reformation were understood. This at length rallied party-feeling on both sides; and the signal for revolution, the red flag of the movement, was *Vestments!* As long as High Church meant only Tracts, it seemed to be without hold over the public imagination; but with the introduction of vestments all England fell into a blaze!

Before the full fury of the No Popery! cry had arisen, Newman was safely over the border; but he left the country perfectly distracted behind him. In Ritualism we have, at once the great glory and the great blot of the system, according to that side of the medal which happens to be turned uppermost. The blot is, that the ceremonies are intended to enforce doctrines and practices generally repudiated by England at the Reformation; but its glory is the glory of revived reverence, decency, and attractiveness of the church services.

The movement had the genius to appropriate to itself the things which appeal to the eye and ear; it consecrated once more the senses to God.

Before we come to Keble as a part of the High Church movement, see well, for your instruction to-night, what are the weak places of that great religious revival, and mark also what must be its enduring strength. The weak places of High Churchism are, 1st, indifference to truth; for it is so passionately devoted to forms and ceremonies that it regards with comparative indifference the facts of history, and the application of common criticism and common sense. It still maintains, in almost all its baldness, the theory of verbal inspiration, or at least the theory of Bible infallibility. Read Christopher Wordsworth's (the present Bishop of Lincoln) Notes to the Four Gospels. It still maintains the almost inspired nature of the Prayer Book, although we all know how parts of that formulary have been wrangled over; and how some parts of it were left, not because they were good and wholesome, but because one faction or the other happened to win. Every scholar knows what a mixed bit of work the Prayer Book is; and yet the Ritualist seems to regard the Romanist portions of the book as inspired almost as the Bible.

Keble finds the greatest comfort in simply going through the church prayers, and says we should hear in each prayer the voice of God himself, that and the voice of God's Church being the same thing. Even here we may admit that it is true to a certain extent of many prayers that they are inspired by the purest devotion; but even this is not to be affirmed of every utterance of the Prayer Book, and I call the assertion that it is so, simply indifference to truth.

2ndly, We have baptismal regeneration, transubstantiation, and similar doctrines. Over each of these things you can dispute, but not one of them will bear the clear light of reason.

Transubstantiation—or that doctrine which does service for it with the Ritualists—was seen to be untrue, and England will never take kindly to it again. But now as ever, men will not live in the spirit; they will have these mystical things to conjure with among the people. The clerical assumption of these supernatural powers is another instance of indifference to truth, and indifference to truth is weakness not strength.

But the clear virtues of the High Church movement are these: it is a visible and symbolic witness of Divine order upon earth; the perception—as against the anarchy of dissent, and the conceit of individualism—that God is a God of order; the correction of the vagaries and caprice of the private conscience, by a fixed, if traditional, system of worship and praise; the conviction that there must be a voice in the church, an orderly hierarchy, a settled administration, a fixed form of service; that unless these things are, confusion and outlawry must result.

And every one of us is benefited by such teaching as this. We have all derived a more settled notion of how we ought to conduct religious services if we wish to infuse life into the Prayer Book. If we wish to know what the Prayer Book means, we must learn to see in it an attempt at least to witness for the visible rule of Christ upon earth.

Then note, further, the patient and exhaustive

way in which the High Church party has appropriated, and revived in the hearts of the people, the teachings of Christ's life, by calling attention to the seasons of the Christian year. How do you suppose that forty years ago I could have ventured to have a choral service like this, without being called a rank Puseyite? Why, forty years ago, and less, clergymen who dressed their choirs in white vestments were called Romanists, and hissed and pelted in the public streets. If they had anything but plain ivy at Christmas about the church, they were called Puseyites; and if they decorated their churches at Easter they would have the school teachers, the churchwardens, and all the influential "old women" of the parish, down upon them. All this went on within my memory. Hear John Henry Newman's account of this matter, together with a crowning tribute to John Keble and the "Christian Year," which will form a fit prelude to our review of it:—

"Much certainly came of the 'Christian Year;' it was the most soothing, tranquillizing, subduing work of the day: if poems can be found to enliven in dejection, and to comfort in anxiety; to cool the over-sanguine, to refresh the weary, and to awe the worldly; to instil resignation into the impatient, and calmness into the fearful and agitated —they are these.

> "Tale tuum carmen nobis, divine poeta,
>   Quale sopor fessis in gramine; quale per æstum
>   Dulcis aquæ saliente sitim restinguere rivo."

Or like the Shepherd's Pipe in the Oriental Vision, of which we are told, that 'the sound was exceedingly sweet, and wrought into a variety of tunes that were inexpressibly melodious, and altogether different from anything I had ever heard. They put me in mind of those heavenly airs which are played to the departing souls of good men upon their first arrival in Paradise, to wear out the impressions of the last agonies, and to qualify them for the pleasures of that place. I drew near with the reverence which is due to a superior nature, and as my heart was entirely subdued by the captivating strains I had heard, I fell down at his feet and wept.'

"Such was the gift of the author of the 'Christian Year;' and he used it in attaching the minds of the rising generation to the church of his predecessors, Ken and Herbert. He did that for the

Church of England which none but a poet could do; he made it poetical. It is sometimes asked whether poets are not more commonly found external to the church than among her children; and it would not surprise us to find the question answered in the affirmative. Poetry is the refuge of those who have not the Catholic Church to flee to, and repose upon; for the church herself is the most sacred and august of poets. Poetry, as Mr. Keble lays it down in his University lectures on the subject, is a method of relieving the over-burdened mind. It is a channel through which emotion finds expression, and that a safe regulated expression. Now what is the Catholic Church, viewed in her human aspect, but a discipline of the affections and passions? What are her ordinances and practices, but the regulated expression of keen, or deep, or turbid feeling, and thus a 'cleansing,' as Aristotle would word it, of the sick soul? She is the poet of her children; full of music to soothe the sad, and control the wayward; wonderful in story for the imagination of the romantic; rich in symbol and imagery, so that gentle and delicate feelings, which will not bear words, may in silence intimate their presence, or commune with themselves. Her very being is poetry; every psalm, every petition, every collect, every versicle, the cross, the mitre, the thurible, is a fulfilment of some dream of childhood, or aspiration of youth. Such poets as are born under her shadow, she takes into her service; she sets them to write hymns, or to compose chants, to embellish shrines, or to determine ceremonies, or to marshal processions; nay, she can even make schoolmen of them, as she made of St. Thomas, till logic becomes poetical. Now the author of the 'Christian Year' found the Anglican system all but destitute of this Divine element, which is an essential property of Catholicism; a ritual dashed upon the ground, trodden on, and broken piecemeal; prayers clipped, pieced, torn, shuffled about at pleasure, until the meaning of the composition perished, and offices which had been poetry were no longer even good prose; antiphons, hymns, benedictions, invocations, shovelled away; Scripture lessons turned into chapters; heaviness, feebleness, unwieldiness, where the Catholic rites had had the lightness and airiness of a spirit; vestments chucked off, lights quenched, jewels stolen, the pomp and circumstances of worship annihilated; a dreariness which could be felt, and which seemed the token of an incipient Socinianism, forcing itself upon the eye, the ear, the nostrils, of the worshipper, as smell of dust and damp, not of incense; a sound of ministers preaching Catholic prayers, and parish clerks droning out Catholic canticles; the royal arms for the crucifix; ugly huge boxes of wood, sacred to preachers, frowning upon the congregation in the place of the mysterious altar; and the long cathedral aisles unused, railed off like the tombs (as they were) of what had been, and was not; and for orthodoxy, a frigid, inelastic, inconsistent, dull, helpless, dogmatic, which could give no just account of·itself, yet was intolerant of all teaching which contained a doctrine more, or a doctrine less, and resented every attempt to give it a meaning:—such was the religion of which this gifted author was, not the judge and denouncer (a deep spirit of reverence hindered it), but the renovator, so far as it has been renovated. Clear as was his perception of the degeneracy of his times, he attributed nothing of it to his church, over which he threw the poetry of his own mind, and the memory of better days.

"His happy magic made the Anglican Church seem what Catholicism was and is. The established system found to its surprise, that it had been all its life talking, not prose, but poetry.

'Miraturque novas frondes, et non sua poma.'

"Beneficed clergymen used to go to rest as usual on Christmas-eve, and leave to ringers, or sometimes to carollers, the observance which was paid, not without creature comforts, to the sacred night; but now they suddenly found themselves, to their great surprise, to be 'wakeful shepherds;' and 'still as the day came round,' 'in music and in light,' the new-born Saviour 'dawned upon their prayer.' Anglican bishops had not only lost the habit of blessing, but had sometimes been startled and vexed when asked to do so; but now they were told of their 'gracious arm stretched out to bless;' moreover, what they had never dreamed when they were gazetted or did homage, they were taught that each of them was 'an apostle true, a crowned and robed seer.' The parish church had been shut up, except for vestry meetings and occasional services, all days of the year but Sundays, and one or two other sacred days; but church-goers were now assured that 'martyrs and saints' dawned on their way; that the Absolution in the Common Prayer Book was 'the golden key each morn and eve;' and informed, moreover, at a time, too, when the real presence was all but utterly forgotten or denied, of 'the dear feast of Jesus dying, upon that altar ever lying, while angels prostrate fall.' They learned, besides, that what their pastors had spoken of, and churchwardens had used at vestry meetings, as a mere table, was 'the dread altar;' and that 'holy lamps were blazing; perfumed embers quivering bright,' while 'stoled priests minister at them; while the floor was by knees of sinners worn.'

"Such doctrines, coming from one who had such claims on his readers from the weight of his name, the depth of his devotional and ethical tone, and the special gift of consolation, of which his poems themselves were the evidence, wrought a great work in the Establishment. The Catholic Church speaks for itself; the Anglican needs external assistance: his poems became a sort of comment upon its formularies and ordinances, and almost elevated them into the dignity of a religious system. It kindled hearts towards his church; it gave a something for the gentle and forlorn to cling to; and it raised up advocates for it among those who otherwise, if God and their good angel had suffered it, might have wandered away into some sort of philosophy, and acknowledged no church at all. Such was the influence of Keble's 'Christian Year.'"[1]

Can we not then turn to our High Church brethren and claim some common ground? Can we not say, It is owing to you that the love of piety has spread again within the church; and we, who do not agree with your doctrines, and think you overstate this and understate that, still desire to take the best things you can give us, and to thank you for them, and not pretend that we have discovered them ourselves. It is true we cannot, like you, denounce the Reformation as something little less than a national disaster. We cannot, like you, long to sit once more at the feet of our dear father the Pope. Because we see how, century after century, the church has blundered, we cannot, like you, always accept its dictation, as defined by your favourite pastors, as inspired—still less as in-

[1] Essays, Crit. and Hist., vol. ii. p. 441.

fallible. But we can join you in your deep reverence for holy things and places—in your desire to revivify what is good in the Prayer Book; we can bear with you when you accuse us of ignorance, or indifference to a theology which, after all, I for one was brought up in, and which no thoughtful and candid person should ignore or reject without examination ; and we follow you, though not in every detail, in your general sense of order and discipline, without surrendering the invisible witness of God in the converted hearts, which, after all, was the gift of your great Low Church predecessors in the Church of England.

This, then, is some account of the good work of the Oxford school : without losing the personal piety and devotion of the Evangelicals, they have greater love for law and order, and they have added to this the glory of practical Christlike activity amongst the poor. They have worked nobly according to their lights in the highways and hedges, in the bye-ways and alleys, of our land ; their schools, their sisterhoods, their parochial agencies, present often admirable examples, fit for general imitation wherever a parish has to be organized; and if the zeal of God's house sometimes eats up the High Church priest, no one can say that he neglects, in season and out of season, to feed Christ's lambs with the best food he has got. Low Church! Broad Church! can you say as much?

Now Keble, according to Newman, was the poet of the movement; he showed that it was beautiful as well as holy; he shed the enthusiasm of a pure and poetic soul over the rigid ceremonial, and flooded the austerity of the Christian seasons with the sacred glow of immeasurable love and pathos. And this is why he has laid hold of English hearts and homes; and the proof of it is that you can go to any railway bookstall in the land, and buy the "Christian Year" for a shilling.

It is out of such a copy, bought thus, that I read to-night. I say that this is the greatest proof of Keble's wide popularity; and this he has achieved, not by dwelling exclusively on those points which divide heart from heart, and inflame earnest minds to bitter differences, but by exalting in the Oxford movement what is universally beautiful and true—the order, the devotion, the imagination, and steady enthusiasm. He has kindled the

Prayer Book into life again; he has clothed again with the heat of piety, and with the blossoms of poetry, the sacred seasons of the Christian year!

III. KEBLE'S POETRY.—Now mark one sign of a poet's influence, in the number of his words and phrases which have worked themselves into the heart of contemporary language. With how many of his words are we familiar! This, no doubt, is partly because his works have been adopted as popular hymns; but they have been so adopted because they are so popular.

> "There is a book, who runs may read,
>   Which heavenly truth imparts;
> And all the lore its scholars need,
>   Pure eyes and Christian hearts.
>
> The works of God, above, below,
>   Within us and around,
> Are pages in that book, to show
>   How God Himself is found."

And the reason why sentences like these work themselves into the heart of the people, is that they contain some universal truth, that comes home to all. And what is the truth in these lines? It is the great doctrine of natural religion —the perception that God and mind live and love throughout the visible universe. And such a truth, ever evanescent yet ever recurrent amongst men, finds here a devotional expression congenial to the age. Was it ever more needed?

Again,

> "'Twas but a little drop of sin
> We saw this morning enter in,
> And lo! at eventide the world was drowned."

That holds you for the same reason. It proclaims the infinite importance of the infinitely little—a truth of science as well as of morals; a truth ever neglected, ever self-asserting—the neglect of little things, the significance of small beginnings. People say "It is nought, it is nought;" but it is the

> "Little pitted speck in garner'd fruit,
> That, rotting inward, slowly moulders all."

It is

> "The little rift within the lute,
> That by-and-by will make the music mute;"

the plague-spot, before the plague; the cloud like a man's hand, before the hurricane; the little cough, which heralds in the rapid consumption; the drop of rain, before the deluge.

And who amongst us has not neglected the insidious approach of sin? Who has not neglected the little things, which, increased, presently threaten the ruin both of mind and body?

Take another example:

> "Not even the tenderest heart, and next our own,
> Knows half the reasons why we smile or sigh."

Yes! think of the deep solitude of the spirit! Is it not true that your best friend knows very little about you? Is it not true that you have an instinctive habit of concealing the innermost things? You cannot give them up. The people who live with you know little or nothing about you in those silent unexplored soul regions; as Emerson has it, "An unnavigable ocean washes between all souls."

No doubt we yield different sides of ourselves to different persons, and indeed, at different times we act and speak very differently in our confidences with the same person. I cannot yield to you that which you cannot command. I cannot hold back from you that which you, and perhaps you alone, have power to draw from me; but the most you, or any one, will ever get of that sacred private thing, my personality, is but a part —a broken light. So—

"Not even the tenderest heart, and next our own,
Knows half the reasons why we smile or sigh."

Perhaps Keble is better known to you in the adapted hymns, or long fragments of his poems, sung in church. In adapting his poems to hymn purposes, we sometimes omit some of those striking passages which are less appropriate for singing than reading; yet in some of these strains Keble seems to have a special glow of inspiration resting upon him, half imaginative, half devotional; and thus we often find a choice gem that precedes what is sung, and which is never printed in our hymn books. That was one reason why the poet himself objected to his hymns being sung. He knew that the singable parts were generally imbedded in a portion which was not singable, and he objected to seeing a connected work cut up for hymn book needs. But the world has its own instincts, and deals rather roughly with authors' thoughts and feelings about their own works. The people are the best judges, after all, of what they want, and they will take it if they can get it.

It is interesting to know that Keble objected to have his things sung; but that is no reason why we should not sing them. Here, then, in one and the same hymn is a specimen of what is sung and of what is not sung.

(*Unsung.*)
"'Tis gone, that bright and orbèd blaze:
Fast fading from our wistful gaze,
Yon mantling cloud has hid from sight
The last faint pulse of quivering light.

In darkness and in weariness
The traveller on his way must press,
No gleam to watch on tree or tower,
Whiling away the lonesome hour."

The singing begins here with the following almost unexampled burst of eloquent fervour:

"Sun of my soul! Thou Saviour dear!
It is not night when Thou art near.
Oh may no earthborn cloud arise
To hide Thee from Thy servant's eyes."

I know no hymn beginning with a grander strain of thoughtful, imaginative contemplation and rising so suddenly to such a climax of ecstasy, as though the Sun of Righteousness itself had suddenly burst upon the darkened spirit, and scattered the gloom of night.

Nor is the Morning Hymn, which is introduced

by a similarly unsingable passage, less dear and less familiar to us all. Indeed, in his own words—

> "As for some dear familiar strain
> Untired we ask, and ask again;
> Ever in its melodious store
> Finding a spell, unheard before."

Even so, as the oft-repeated words fall upon our willing ears, and warm our hearts:

> "New every morning is the love
> Our wakening and uprising prove,
> Through sleep and darkness safely brought,
> Restored to life, and power, and thought.
>
> * * * * *
>
> If on our daily course our mind
> Be set to hallow all we find,
> New treasures still, of countless price,
> God will provide for sacrifice.
>
> Old friends, old scenes, will lovelier be
> As more of heaven in each we see:
> Some softening gleam of love and prayer
> Shall dawn on every cross and care.
>
> * * * * *
>
> We need not bid, for cloister'd cell,
> Our neighbour and our work farewell,
> Nor strive to wind ourselves too high
> For sinful man beneath the sky:

> The trivial round, the common task,
> Would furnish all we ought to ask;
> Room to deny ourselves; a road
> To bring us, daily, nearer God.
>
> Seek we no more; content with these,
> Let present rapture, comfort, ease,
> As heaven shall bid them, come and go:—
> The secret this of rest below.
>
> Only, O Lord, in Thy dear love
> Fit us for perfect rest above;
> And help us, this and every day,
> To live more nearly as we pray."

We find in Keble the most piercing glimpses into the interior life, reminding us of the ecstasy or meditation of some old saint, dreaming in the cloister, or beside the crucifix in the retired cell; it is Paul with the thorn in the flesh; it is Cyprian awaiting martyrdom; it is Perpetua, or Felicité, or St. Catherine, wrapt in quiet contemplation in the midst of torment, reposing in the everlasting arms.

> "Oh Lord my God, do Thou Thy holy will
>   I will be still;
> I will not stir, lest I forsake thine arm,
>   And break the charm
> Which lulls me, clinging to my Father's breast,
>   In perfect rest.

> Wild Fancy, peace! thou must not me beguile
>   With thy false smile;
> I know thy flatteries, and thy cheating ways.
>   Be silent, Praise!
> Blind guide with siren voice, and blinding all
>   That hear thy call.
> Come, Self-Devotion! high and pure
> Thoughts that in thankfulness endure,
> Though dearest hopes are faithless found,
> And dearest hearts are bursting round.
> Come, Resignation! spirit meek,
> And let me kiss thy placid cheek."

We find also, as we might expect, peculiar fragments on the association with holy places. Very much of the life of the High Church movement depended on such association—on saying your prayers at particular places and at particular times, or on confessing to particular priests. It is a thing too much neglected by Christian people—this power of locality, person, time, and place. Keble says somewhere, If you cannot go to church, make a church in your house; let there be some little room or corner, where you may go for the associations of prayer, and see if you will not pray better when you pray regularly in the same place. This feeling of association is raised to its highest power in poems where the poet transports himself to the very spot in the garden of Gethsemane where the Lord saw the angel, and prayed that if it were possible the cup might pass from Him.

> "There is a spot within this sacred dale
> That felt Thee kneeling, touched Thy prostrate brow.
> One angel knows it : O might prayer avail
> To win the knowledge, sure each holy vow
> Less quickly from the unstable soul would fade,
> Offer'd where Christ in agony was laid."

There is also a passage where he deals with Moses, bringing the universal feeling of religion out of the remote heart of antiquity, and making it glow with the historical association. It is not Moses the lawgiver, but the shepherd; and I do think that Keble when he wrote this hymn must have seen that picture of Signorelli's, on the wall of the Sistine Chapel, at Rome, where Moses, the shepherd of Jethro's flocks, is seen kneeling apart in the wilderness, in prayer, with his face upturned as if he saw a vision. He is far away from the sheep, and utterly absorbed; it is the face of one who sees God.

> "Far seen across the sandy wild,
> There like a solitary child
> He thoughtless roam'd, and free;

> One towering thorn was wrapp'd in flame,
> Bright without blaze it went and came;
> Who would not turn to see?
>
> Along the mountain ledges green
> The scatter'd sheep at will may glean
> The desert's spicey stores;
> *The while with undivided heart*
> *The shepherd talks to God apart,*
> *And whilst he talks adores.*"

The italics are ours.

I might dwell at length upon the various beauties of Keble's style—his flowing music, his perfect lines, such as his apostrophe to Christ on His desertion by Peter,—

> "Thou thrice denied, yet thrice beloved,
> Watch by Thine own forgiven friend."

Or the beautiful description of those who, like Paul, would fain depart, and yet are willing to bide their time—

> "Waiting their summons to the sky,
> Content to live, but not afraid to die."

Or that tender passage—the reflection of his own experience of human love, as we learn from his biography—where the human passion is pressed into the service of the heavenly love. Take, as an illustration,—

"Who ever saw the earliest rose
    First open her sweet breast?
Or, when the summer sun goes down,
The first soft star in evening's crown
    Light up her gleaming crest?

Fondly we seek the dawning bloom
    On features wan and fair,—
The gazing eye no change can trace;
But look away a little space,
    Then turn, and, lo! 'tis there.

But there's a sweeter flower than e'er
    Blush'd on the rosy spray—
A brighter star, a richer bloom
Than e'er did western heaven illume
    At close of summer day.

'Tis Love, the last best gift of heaven;
    Love, gentle, holy, pure;
But, tenderer than a dove's soft eye,
The searching sun, the open sky,
    She never could endure.

Even human Love will shrink from sight
    Here in the coarse rude earth;
How then should rash intruding glance
Break in upon *her* sacred trance
    Who boasts a heavenly birth?

So still and secret is her growth.
    Ever the truest heart:
Where deepest strikes her kindly root
For hope or joy, for flower or fruit,
    Least knows the happy part.

> God only, and good angels, look
>   Behind the blissful screen—
> As when, triumphant o'er His woes,
> The Son of God by moonlight rose,
>   By all but Heaven unseen."

Or again, in such pure poetical passages as this, where the light grace of Moore is mingled with the more pensive delicacy and earnestness of Bryant:

> "Since all that is not Heaven must fade,
>   Light be the hand of Ruin laid
>   Upon the home I love:
> With lulling spell let soft Decay
> Steal on, and spare the giant sway,
>   The crash of tower and grove.
>
> Far opening down some woodland deep
> In their own quiet glade should sleep
>   The relics dear to thought,
> And wild-flower wreaths from side to side
> Their waving tracery hang, to hide
>   What ruthless Time has wrought."

I consider that there are about three poems, taken as wholes, in which Keble rises in different ways to his full height. I cite them as examples without a weak line and without a poor thought—conceived at high pressure, and executed without a flaw or blemish. A man of the best quality will do this two or three times in his life. Keble has done it in "St. John," "Balaam," and "Christ's Agony on the Cross." I will give first the "St. John :"

> "'Lord, and what shall this man do?'
>   Ask'st thou, Christian, for thy friend?
> If his love for Christ be true,
>   Christ hath told thee of his end:
> This is he whom God approves,
> This is he whom Jesus loves.
>
> Ask not of him more than this,
>   Leave it in his Saviour's breast,—
> Whether, early call'd to bliss,
>   He in youth shall find his rest;
> Or armed in his station wait
> Till his Lord be at the gate:
>
> Whether in his lonely course
>   (Lonely, not forlorn) he stay,
> Or with Love's supporting force
>   Cheat the toil and cheer the way:
> Leave it all in His high hand
> Who doth hearts as streams command.
>
> Gales from heaven, if so He will,
>   Sweeter melodies can wake
> On the lonely mountain rill
>   Than the meeting waters make.
> Who hath the Father and the Son,
> May be left, but not alone.

> Sick or healthful, slave or free,
>   Wealthy, or despised and poor—
> What is that to him or thee,
>   So his love to Christ endure?
> When the shore is won at last,
> Who will count the billows past?
>
> Only, since our souls will shrink
>   At the touch of natural grief,
> When our earthly loved ones sink,
>   Lend us, Lord, Thy sure relief;
> Patient hearts, their pain to see,
> And Thy grace, to follow Thee."

I will next produce "Balaam;" but remember that, whenever you read a poem of this kind, at once devotional, historical, and imaginative, you must have the whole of the subject in your memory and in your mind's eye. Keble always supposes that you know your Bible; and in reading this following poem of "Balaam" you must have the whole of the history before you, and then the poem will be like the music to that incomparable drama —then you will find it perfect throughout, full, but not surcharged with ideas; ingenious, yet clear, pressing every incident into its service. Before I read the poem, let the view of Balaam's dealings with Balak pass before you.

First, the summons sent by the king to Balaam,

when he invited him to curse the people of Israel; then Balaam's eagerness to go; God's veto, "Thou shalt not go down;" then Balaam's attempt to extort an unwilling consent from God, lusting in his soul after the gold and the silver of Balak; then remember how at last his prayer is granted in wrath, as God often seems to grant our impetuous and peevish petitions in wrath when they are not good for us; then remember the angel in the narrow path of the vineyard, with a drawn sword, and the refusal of the ass to go on, and Balaam's rage; then his arrival, the meeting and colloquy between Balak and Balaam—Balaam feeling himself powerless to please Balak, reluctantly true to his prophetic mission, refusing to commit himself to cursing the people of God, declaring "what God puts in my mouth, that only will I speak," and yet all the time longing to curse; then the successive bursts of prophecy, finishing with the vision of the Messiah—" I shall see Him, but not now; I shall behold Him, but not nigh. There shall come a star out of Jacob, and a sceptre shall arise out of Israel, and shall smite the corners of Moab, and destroy all the children of Sheth."

With this history already moving before your eyes like so many pictures, come we to the poem:

> "O for a sculptor's hand!
> That thou might'st take thy stand,
> Thy wild hair floating on the eastern breeze,
> Thy tranced yet open gaze
> Fix'd on the desert haze,
> As one who deep in heaven some airy pageant sees!
> In outline dim and vast
> Their fearful shadows cast,
> The giant forms of Empires on their way
> To ruin: one by one
> They tower, and they are gone:
> Yet in the Prophet's soul the dreams of avarice stay.
> No sun or star so bright
> In all the world of light
> That they should draw to heaven his downward eye:
> He hears th' Almighty's word,
> He sees the angel's sword,
> Yet low upon the earth his heart and treasure lie.
>
> * * * * *
>
> We in the tents abide
> Which he at distance eyed
> Like goodly cedars by the waters spread,
> While seven red altar-fires
> Rose up in wavy spires
> Where on the mount he watch'd his sorceries dark and dread.
> He watch'd till morning's ray
> On lake and meadow lay,
> And willow-shaded streams, that silent sweep

    Around the banner'd lines,
      Where by their several signs
The desert-wearied tribes in sight of Canaan sleep.

    He watch'd, till knowledge came
      Upon his soul like flame—
Not of those magic fires at random caught;
      But true Prophetic light
      Flash'd o'er him, high and bright—
Flash'd once, and died away, and left his darken'd thought.

    And can he choose but fear,
      Who feels his God so near
That, when he fain would curse, his powerless tongue,
      In blessing only moves?
      Alas! the world he loves
Too close around his heart her tangling veil hath flung.

    Sceptre and Star divine,
      Who in Thine inmost shrine
Hast made us worshippers, O claim Thine own;
      More than Thy seers we know—
      O teach our love to grow
Up to Thy heavenly light, and reap what Thou hast sown."

Here is one concluding poem, in which I think Keble rises to even a higher level of continuous inspiration. We have before us the spectacle of Christ upon the Cross: He is offered the anodyne of myrrh, and refuses to drink, preferring to suffer the extreme agonies of the cross. I suppose the words are put into the mouth of some disciple, who is eagerly longing that the Lord should be spared some pain:

"'Fill high the bowl, and spice it well, and pour
    The dews oblivious: for the Cross is sharp,
        The Cross is sharp, and He
        Is tenderer than a lamb.

'He wept by Lazarus' grave—how will He bear
    This bed of anguish? and His pale weak form
        Is worn with many a watch
        Of sorrow and unrest.

'His sweat last night was as great drops of blood;
    And the sad burthen press'd Him so to earth,
        The very torturers paused
        To help Him on His way.

'Fill high the bowl, benumb His aching sense
    With medicined sleep.'—O awful in Thy woe!
        The parching thirst of death
        Is on Thee, and Thou triest

The slumb'rous potion bland—and wilt not drink:
Not sullen, nor in scorn, like haughty man
        With suicidal hand
        Putting his solace by:

But as at first Thine all-pervading look
Saw from Thy Father's bosom to th' abyss,
        Measuring in calm presage
        The infinite descent;

So to the end, though now of mortal pangs
Made heir, and emptied of thy glory awhile,
    With unaverted eye
    Thou meetest all the storm.

Thou wilt feel all, that Thou may'st pity all;
And rather would'st Thou wrestle with strong pain
    Than overcloud Thy soul,
    So clear in agony,

Or lose one glimpse of heaven before the time.
O, most entire and perfect sacrifice,
    Renew'd in every pulse
    That on the tedious cross

Told the long hours of death, as, one by one,
The life-strings of that tender heart gave way.
    E'en sinners, taught by Thee,
    Look sorrow in the face,

And bid her freely welcome, unbeguiled
By false kind solaces and spells of earth;—
    And yet not all unsoothed;
    For when was joy so dear

As the deep calm that breathed 'Father forgive,'
Or, 'Be with me in Paradise to-day?'
    And though the strife be sore,
    Yet in his parting breath

Love masters agony; the soul that seem'd
Forsaken, feels her present God again,
    And in her Father's arms
    Contented dies away.

VII.

George Herbert.

SELECTED POEMS.

VII.

George Herbert.

SELECTED POEMS.

WE could scarcely have found a greater contrast than that presented by George Herbert and Keble, yet it is one which, while it separates, yet draws these men together. The one is the typical churchman of the Elizabethan, the other of the Victorian age. But Keble is without Herbert's humour, and Herbert is without Keble's emotion. The one is the austere Puritan, the other glows with Roman Catholic fervour. Each embodies with fervid piety the influence which happened at the time to be passing over the Church of England.

With George Herbert we come upon the great age when the English language became substantially what it now is. Our language possessed then a certain directness of expression, which we are in some danger of losing. German, and French, and Italian have since grown common in England,

and consequently many words of foreign extraction have been introduced into the English language; and although this has doubtless enriched our tongue, yet it has been thought that we are in danger of thereby losing something of our native force and directness of expression.

In the old days men neither wrote nor spoke so much as they do now, but they wrote and spoke very much to the purpose; hence there is a wonderful and condensed force and vigour in the language of Shakespeare, Milton, and George Herbert; and the translators of our Bible, the framers of our Liturgy, shared these gifts. For this reason I do not wish to see a new translation, or a new Prayer Book, because the old ones belong to the classic age of English literature.

Between Shakespeare (1564) and Milton (1608), as between two suns of surpassing brilliancy, lie a host of minor poets—stars of lesser magnitude—but not for that reason to be overlooked.

Indeed the Elizabethan age is best read by the light of the Elizabethan poets, and an age so complex needs all the light that can be thrown upon it. Perhaps at no time since England had become a nation was there such a strange and sudden fusion of old and new ideas.

Through the printing-press books got to be numerous beyond all precedent, and the middle-age giant of popular ignorance lay sick unto death.

Through the discovery of the Bible to the million, the phantom of Roman Catholic superstition had been, if not laid, at all events considerably dwarfed.

Through the revival of art and literature in Italy, English taste had been reached, and quickened into new life. Music, painting, architecture, and classical study were national pursuits.

Piratical enterprise brought to light new aspects of life in Africa and America, whilst commercial enterprise opened up new avenues of wealth. The English navy established for a time our supremacy by sea, whilst the fortunate issue of internal war and intrigue ended in the union of Scotland and England under one crown.

That such changes could go on without materially affecting the government of the country, was hardly to be expected. Popular religion and popular education invariably precede a cry for popular government. But between the two great struggles in England there came a pause. Elizabeth's successor, James I. of England and VI. of Scotland, occupied that short space of time between the great religious and the great political revolutions. The Reformation of Henry VIII. was passed; the Protectorate of Oliver Cromwell had not yet arrived. It would be an interesting study to trace the above-mentioned various and exciting influences as they appear reflected in that great burst of song which marks what we call the Elizabethan period. With a kind of feverish activity the poets of the time seemed to embrace everything in heaven and earth.

Shakespeare reigns supreme in the kingdom of human nature; he is followed by a host of dramatists. Spenser discourses sweetly in the language of mythology and symbolism, standing alone in the profusion of his imagery, the melody of his verse, and the incomparable vigour and lightness of his fancy. After him we have poets treating on every secular subject, and reflecting every phase of thought and feeling, as in Phineas and Giles Fletcher, extending down to simple geography, as in the case of Michael Drayton. Then there are poets half religious, half secular, such as Donne; witty, sentimental, pious, by turns, neat in epigrams, eloquent in epitaphs. Yet not even Donne presents such a strange mixture as good Sir John

Davies, whose two best known works are a poem on "Dancing," and another on the "Immortality of the Soul."

The purely religious spirit is never in any age long in the background, and in the midst of these conflicting elements it kept steadily to the front; the new wine of the Reformation entered into everything; every educated person knew the points in dispute—had strong religious opinions; most read their Bibles with avidity; and speculations on doctrine, often at the expense of practice, were unusually rife. Religious truth and the religious life were subjects of universal interest, and it would have been strange indeed if they had not found their poets. The best, the wisest, the quaintest, the most holy of them all, was George Herbert.

Partly a consequence of, partly a protest against, a theology-loving age, he was constantly calling men back from subtleties to saintliness, from doctrinal theology to practical religion; but as the mind and method of the man will best be seen in his life and works, we present the reader with a few details of the one, and a few notes and extracts from the other.

I. LIFE OF GEORGE HERBERT.—George was the fifth son of Richard Herbert, a descendant of the famous William Herbert, Earl of Pembroke, who lived in the reign of Edward IV. He was born on the 3rd of April, 1593, in Montgomery Castle, near the town of that name. The castle belonged to his family, but passed out of their hands during the Great Rebellion, and was laid level with the dust a few years afterwards.

His mother, Magdalen, who also came of a distinguished family—the Newports—was one of the most accomplished women of the age. She numbered amongst her intimate friends Sir Henry Wotton and Dr. Donne; and the latter ingenious divine has left us many records of her piety, intellect, and beauty. He writes—and there can be no doubt of whom—

> "No spring nor summer beauty has such grace
> As I have seen in an autumnal face.
> In all her words, to every hearer fit,
> You may at revels or at council sit."

This admirable woman exercised an extraordinary influence over all her children; and as she was left a widow when little George was only four years old, she had to use her discretion in moulding one of the gentlest, but at the same time one of the keenest and most original, minds of that time. George passed, at the age of twelve, to Westminster School, where he attracted the attention of his masters by his precocious wit and extraordinary facility for the classics; he also won the hearts of his schoolfellows by his warm and generous nature, and his sweet and genial manners. At fifteen, having gained a King's Scholarship, he was elected for Trinity College, Cambridge, and settled there about 1608. His mother, who had followed his brother to college, and taken up her abode near the town, does not seem to have been so anxious about George. She had, however, warned him that " our souls do insensibly take in vice by the example or conversation with wicked company, and that the very knowledge of wickedness was as tinder to inflame and kindle sin, and keep it burning." And George in his turn soon proved that her counsels were not bestowed in vain. In his first year at Cambridge he writes to her his indignation at the many love poems that were daily writ and consecrated to Venus, bewailing that so few were writ that looked towards God and heaven; and concludes with the following memorable words: "For my own part, my meaning, dear mother, is in these sonnets (enclosed) to declare my resolution to be that my poor abilities in poetry shall be all and ever consecrated to God's glory."

At this time he had no intention of entering the church; yet thus early and thus half-unconsciously was the key-note of his future greatness struck. He graduated in 1611, was made Fellow of his college in 1615, and became Public Orator in 1619.

And now it must be said that at this time George Herbert was fond of fine clothes, particular in his associates, proud of his family, distant though not uncourteous to his inferiors, and was thought to have the finest manners of any in the University. He so ably discharged the elegant functions of Orator, which consisted chiefly in making suitable Latin speeches in the presence of the University whenever degrees were conferred or great people had to be eulogized, that he attracted before long the attention of James I., himself a scholar and writer of some pretensions. The two found each other's society so congenial, that Mr. Herbert began to desert University life for the Court, and indeed was constantly in attendance on the King.

Sir Francis Bacon, "the great secretary of nature and all learning," courted his acquaintance; and good Bishop Andrews so admired him, that he carried about him a letter in Greek from Herbert to the last day of his life. And amongst other powerful friends we may here mention the Duke of Richmond and the Marquis of Hamilton.

Visions of earthly glory now rose before him. He found the University disagreed with him. Politics seemed a larger sphere, more suited to his taste and capacities; he had a ready wit and a subtle mind, and looked forward to occupying some high position in the State; but "God disposes." The glittering prospect opened but to close. Suddenly all his most powerful friends seemed to die or be taken away from him. The Duke of Richmond, and then the Marquis of Hamilton, and shortly afterwards his great patron, the king, were stricken down by his side; and he found himself in a changed Court, with a king that knew him not, and alien faces around him.

Whether about this time he grew tired of worldly vanities, saw the hollowness of earthly ambitions, or could not stoop to become one of a crowd of new and obsequious courtiers, it is not easy to say; but most probably his deeply religious nature, which had been partially swamped by the pleasures and ambitions of Court life, now arose in its might, and clamoured for that supremacy which it speedily acquired, and which it so firmly retained to the close. He retired into the country, gave up, apparently not without a struggle, the prospects of a political career, and was for some time much unsettled and disturbed in his mind. He desired above all things to be useful:—

> "Now I am here, what wilt Thou do with me
> None of my books will show;
> I read and sigh—I wish I were a tree,
> For then sure I should grow."

But he discovered that his genius was above all religious, and that no sphere which did not bring him into constant contact with spiritual things would really meet the requirements of his soul. He must serve man, but he must serve God, and what tastes he had must be pressed into their service, not paraded for their own sakes. All attempts to rest in them were vain: "other lords may have had dominion over him," but their time was now passed.

He who had looked forward to being made

Secretary of State was now only ambitious to take holy orders; and to a Court friend, who rebuked him for desiring an occupation so far below his birth and great talents, he made the following beautiful reply: "It hath been formerly judged that the domestic servants of the King of Heaven should be of the noblest families on earth; and though the iniquity of late times hath made clergymen meanly valued, and the sacred name of priest contemptible, yet I will labour to make it honourable by consecrating all my learning and all my poor abilities to advance the glory of that God that gave them. And I will labour to be like my Saviour, by making humility lovely in the eyes of all men, and by following the merciful and meek example of my dear Jesus."

Thus chastened in spirit, he entered upon the small incumbency of Layton Ecclesia, in the diocese of Lincoln, in 1626.

He found the church nearly in ruins, and with characteristic energy resolved to rebuild it. He was not rich, and could only look about him for richer friends to help him. His mother's counsel was for once disregarded. "George," she said, "it is not for your weak body and empty purse to undertake to build churches." But Herbert answered with all respect, that he had made a vow to God to rebuild the church; and with the assistance of his liberal friends, the Duke of Lennox, Sir Henry Herbert, Mr. Nicholas Farrer, and some few others, he was able to perform the task.

Isaak Walton tells us that he made the reading-desk and pulpit both the same height, "because," said he, " prayer and preaching, being equally useful, should agree like brethren, and have an equal honour and estimation." In 1629, and in the thirty-fourth year of his age, he was seized with a sharp quotidian ague. His sufferings were at times intense, and he would often cry out, "Lord, abate my great affliction or increase my patience;" and finding the doctor's remedies of little use, he began to cure himself by nearly total abstinence from everything except a little salt meat. Being now reduced to great weakness, his friends vied with each other in providing him with change of air and every comfort. Lord Danvers loved him so dearly that he had rooms set apart at Dauntsey Hall, Wiltshire, and there Mr. Herbert enjoyed perfect rest, moderate study, and much delightful social intercourse. Here he fell in with a near relation of the Earl's, one Mr. Danvers, who counselled him to marry, and indeed offered him every facility, for he himself had nine daughters, and openly declared that he would like no one better than Mr. Herbert for a son-in-law.

Jane appears to have been the favourite; and hearing so much of Mr. Herbert, she grew to love him, when her father suddenly died, and the family circle was thrown into confusion. But they who had hitherto seen little of each other, and had been lovers in theory and after quite a Platonic fashion, were now to grow into a more dear and intimate relationship. In a very little time Jane became the wife of George Herbert, whose health and spirits seemed greatly to revive, and not long afterwards he was presented to his last living, Bemerton, in Wiltshire, and prepared to take priest's orders.

He had now but three years more to live, and he entered upon this last brief period with as much solemn preparation and earnest prayer as if he had known that the night was coming in which no man could work.

At his induction, according to custom he was shut into Bemerton Church to toll the bell. His friends waited for him at the church door. The bell had long ceased, but still Herbert did not appear. His friends grew anxious, and knocked and knocked again without success. At last his dear friend Mr. Woodnot stepped round, and peeped in at the chancel window, and there he saw Mr. Herbert lying on the altar-steps, not insensible, but absorbed in deep devotion. It was then and there that he made certain rules for the discipline and management of his future life, and many of them may be found in "The Country Parson," under the headings, "The Parson's Knowledge," "The Parson on Sundays," "The Parson Arguing," "The Parson with his Churchwardens," "The Parson in his Mirth," &c.

On the same night it was noticed that he was unusually light-hearted and serene, and conversing freely with Mr. Woodnot, he said, "I now look back upon my aspiring thoughts, and think myself more happy than if I had attained what then I so thirsted for." He was often heard to say that he knew the ways of learning; knew what nature does willingly, and what when it is forced by fire; knew the ways of honour, and when glory inclines the soul to noble expressions; knew the Court; knew the ways of pleasure; and upon what terms he declined all these for the service of his Master, Jesus Christ: and he rejoices—

> "That through these labyrinths not my grovelling wit,
>   But Thy silk twist, let down from heaven to me,
> Did both conduct and teach me how by it
>   To climb to Thee."

Mr. Herbert now devoted himself to repair the church and parsonage-house, and both he and his wife were indefatigable in relieving the necessities of their poor.

But the service of God and the cure of souls were ever first in his thoughts. Twice a day the family met in a little chapel close to the parsonage, and the parishioners soon learned to drop in from the fields when they heard the little bell, and joined Mr. Herbert in some of the church prayers.

His love of the Reformed Prayer Book was unbounded, and the whole of his preaching turned upon explaining its various parts, and trying to make that a reasonable and living service which might otherwise degenerate into a dry and formal one. But Herbert felt the prayers himself, and he made his people feel their power. He read them slowly and impressively, pausing occasionally to allow the people to collect their thoughts, and offer up the prayers for themselves.

On Sunday morning he preached, and on Sunday afternoon after the Second Lesson he catechized and instructed from the pulpit; "and," says his quaint biographer, Isaak Walton—perhaps as a sly comment upon certain "learned and painful" ministers—"he never exceeded his half-hour, and was always so happy as to have an obedient and full congregation."

Mr. Herbert's favourite recreation was music, and he often walked to and from Salisbury to attend the meetings of his musical society. On these walks he met friends and parishioners, and never failed to indulge them with profitable advice and elevated counsel. Meeting one day a minister who complained of the lax morals of the laity, Mr. Herbert told him plainly that the remedy was for the clergy to live blameless lives. "This," he continued, "would be a cure for the wickedness and growing atheism of our age. And, my dear brother, till this is done by us, and done in earnest, let no man expect a reformation of the manners of the laity." He was of all men most helpful—he knew how to provide clothing for the poor, food for the hungry—he could lend a hand at the plough, and put his back to an overloaded cart, and never was known to turn his face from any poor man. His conversation was lively and full of wit; and though his own life was blameless, his large knowledge of secular society made him familiar with the sins of all classes, and in his treatment of difficult cases he combined happily the wisdom of the serpent with the innocence of the dove. The quaintest and most homely allusions crept into his sermons, and pointed much of his religious poetry; and he had the singular merit of being plain and personal without vulgarity, gentle without feebleness, and pious without hypocrisy.

Thus loving and beloved, " wearing the white flower of blameless " life, he drew to his close. His constitution, naturally delicate, seemed never to have recovered from the effects of the remedies he used during his severe illness.

His wife noticed with alarm his thinness and

the growing pallor of his thoughtful face. He read prayers with the greatest difficulty. It was plain that consumption was making sure and rapid strides; and when implored to desist from a work which he could no longer really perform, he was fain to say, "I will not be wilful, for though my spirit be willing, yet I find my flesh is weak."

One month before his death came Mr. Duncan, a clergyman, from a dear friend, to see him, and bear back tidings of his condition.

"Sir," said Herbert, "I perceive from your habit that you are a priest, and I desire you to pray with me."

"What prayers?" asked Mr. Duncan.

"Oh, sir, the prayers of my mother the Church of England—no others are equal to them; but I beg of you pray only the Litany, for I am weak and faint."

"His discourse," says the same Duncan, "was so pious, and his motion so genteel and meek, that after almost forty years, yet they remain fresh in my memory."

On hearing of his approaching death, Mr.

Woodnot, the same that had surprised him praying in the chancel, hurried to his bedside; but so great was Mr. Herbert's calm, that sorrow and sighing seemed to flee away from his presence, and his words sounded not so much like those of a dying man, as fragments of heavenly melody chanted on this side the grave; as he lay faint, but filled with divine meditations, he would say, "I now look back upon the pleasures of my life past, and see the content I have taken in beauty, in wit, in pleasant conversation, and all these are now past by me like a dream, or as a shadow that returns not. And my hope is that I shall shortly leave this valley of tears, and be free from all fever and pain, and, which is better, free from sin, and this being past I shall dwell in the New Jerusalem; and this is my content, that I am going daily towards it, and that I shall live the less time for having lived this and the day past." And a little before his death he observed to Mr. Woodnot, "My dear friend, I am sorry I have nothing to present to my merciful God, but sin and misery; but the first is pardoned, and a few hours will now put a period to the latter, for I shall suddenly go hence and be no more seen."

Soon after, he swooned away; but recovering himself, he said to those about his bed, "I have passed a conflict with my last enemy, and have overcome him by the merits of my Master, Jesus."

He then desired his will to be brought, and making Mr. Woodnot his executor, commended unto him his wife and nieces. Then, growing very faint, he was heard to say, "I am now ready to die; Lord, forsake me not now my strength faileth; Lord, Lord, now receive my soul;" and so passed away.

George Herbert died in his thirty-ninth year, and was buried on the 3rd of March, 1632, at Bemerton. His wife survived him many years, and afterwards became the wife of Sir Robert Cook, of Highnam, by whom she had her first and only child, a girl. She died in 1663, and is buried at Highnam.

II. GEORGE HERBERT'S POETRY. — George Herbert was a most eloquent scholar, and wrote a great deal of excellent Latin poetry, but he has won the love of all religious hearts by "The Temple," a collection of poems published after his death, and bearing upon public worship, private devotion, and practical religion.

As a poet, Herbert had many imitators, but no rivals. Tricks of his style and tempers of his mind have been caught with success; but the incomparable mixture of pathos, sublimity, piety, subtlety, quaintness, and common sense, remains unimitated and inimitable. The constant object he had in view was to use poetry for man's good and God's glory, as much as other writers abused it to man's harm and God's dispraise. As another holy man thought it ill that the devil should have all the good tunes, so Herbert would not let him have all the good poems. There is a queer worldly-wise tone about him sometimes, as who should say, "I know your manners, my worldly friends, and I adopt your dialect to catch you." He may write outside "Love songs;" but the love is Divine, not human. He possessed the faculty of expressing Divine truth in an odd way, and the power of pressing everything, however trivial, into the service of Heaven. "The birds that drink and straight lift up their heads," teach us to taste of joy, but look to heavenly things—"the winds and waters here below do flee and flow," like the tempestuous times that "amaze poor mortals"— the flowers of earth tell of the Paradise of God

—the lark's voice becomes a reprover of man, the bees are called on to sting him to industry, and by a ladder of sunbeams he is bid climb up to heaven.

At times, such is the happy confusion of his imagery that heaven and earth seemed interchangeable terms—both paid him wages, and he could often hear—

"Church bells beyond the stars."

We are all by turns taken into his confidence. His soul is often laid bare in its inmost recesses, his struggles are not withheld, his triumphs are not concealed, and he constantly calls us to share in his own sublime hopes and imperishable consolations. Meanwhile, nothing at times can be more quaint and homely than his language; we think he must have spoken just so. He meets us by the way, and begins thinking out loud.

Now he is in the garden, now in the tool-house, now by the wayside, now packing up to go away; anything supplies him with an illustration:

"The most of me to heaven is fled,
My thoughts and joys are all pack'd up and gone."

He has noticed the use of a gimlet, and says—

> "No scrue, no piercer can
>   Into a piece of timber work and winde,
> As God's afflictions into man."

A cupboard with a key in it, unlocked, has caught his eye—

> "Joy, I did lock thee up; but some bad man
> Did let thee out again."

He has noticed wares put out for sale on some shop counter, and tells us that in God's great mart of the world there are "afflictions sorted—anguish of all sizes."

No doubt his poetry attracted many readers of that day by poetical conceits now out of date, but then fashionable. Thus, we have a poem called "Heaven"—

> "O who will show me those delights on high?
>   Echo—I!
> Thou, Echo, thou art mortal, all men know.
>   Echo—No!"

And in another, about Christ, we have—

> "To my broken heart He was *I ease you;*
> And to my whole is *Jesu.*"

And probably the following elegant fancy would not be tolerated in these days. Speaking of the Apostles as lights in the world, he says—

> "The sunne, which once did shine alone,
>   Hung down his head and wished for night,
> When he beheld twelve sunnes for one
>   Going about the world and giving light."

But if at times he was fanciful, he was more often directly practical, and gives us to know our business as probably no other poet before or after has ever done.

When the church bell rings, we are told to hurry off and get in before service begins.

> "Oh, be drest;
> Stay not for the other pin; why, thou hast lost
> A joy for it worth worlds."

And to all spendthrifts he gives counsel:—

> "By no means run in debt; take thine own measure;
>   Who cannot live on twenty pounds a year, cannot on forty."

We have dwelt upon these minor points because his great merits are known to every one. The pathos of "Sacrifice," with its recurring refrain, "Was ever grief like Mine?" has perhaps never been surpassed. The tender grace of "Vertue," better known as "Sweet day, so cool, so calm, so bright," is familiar to all. The little poem of "The Call," short, condensed, and perfect, is less widely known:—

"Come, my Way, my Truth, my Life;
  Such a Way as gives us breath,
Such a Truth as ends all strife,
  Such a Life as killeth death.

Come, my Light, my Feast, my Strength;
  Such a Light as shows us feast,
Such a Feast as mends in length,
  Such a Strength as makes his guest.

Come, my Joy, my Love, my Heart;
  Such a Joy as none can move,
Such a Love as none can part,
  Such a Heart as joyes in love."

Among other poems to be read for ever, we may mention "The Quip," "Businesse," "Love Unknown," and "Discipline." We cite these, not to exclude any, but as being beautiful where all are fair.

Like every true poet, in one way George Herbert belongs to no age, and in another he is the most perfect reflection of his own. We are sometimes reminded of the archaic forms and quaint fun of Chaucer; at others the rich melody and majestic dignity of Milton seems anticipated; whilst again, there are passages which so exactly hit the analytical temper of our own deeply self-conscious age, that it is hard to believe that the author of the "In

Memoriam" has not been directly or indirectly indebted to them.

From what has been said it is evident that George Herbert was a man of great force and individuality; and this is indeed why his poems have retained their popularity. Condensed into that little book, the "Works of George Herbert," are poems which touch upon every part of the Church Service. Here also, human life is passed in brief but graphic review; whilst the duties of a clergyman, as Herbert conceived them, are succinctly laid down. Into this small book is really epitomized the life-work of a great man. Here is power which might have ruled a kingdom. Indeed in the judgment of those who knew him, this quaint poet would have risen high in the State, and aspired to the greatest worldly distinction; but had he done this he would never perhaps have reached so many hearts, or have done so much good to succeeding generations.

I will now summarize certain features or characteristics of George Herbert. Perhaps the first which strikes the reader is his profound attachment to the English Church, and his profound belief in the Book of Common Prayer. The reason was simply this. Both were, to him and his age, new sensations. To us, they are as well-worn and familiar institutions. The church is old, and the Prayer Book, however rehabilitated with high church fervour, is worn. But imagine the feelings of an ardent churchman in those days towards the Bible in the English tongue, and the National Church of England, newly freed from Romish fetters, lifeless forms, and oppressive taxes.

Suddenly, the Latin mumblings of priests—often unintelligible to themselves, mostly inaudible to the people—cease; the prayers of the church are put into English, and the Bible is restored to the people in the vulgar tongue; thousands read for the first time its wondrous narratives; the clergy encourage and assist in the perusal; once more the church gives literature and education to the new world, as the Roman Catholic Church gave it to the old world which had passed away for ever; the sermons become living, instead of dry, formal, and scholastic; the public offices of religion are transformed, and tawdry decoration makes way for glowing faith, the sense yielding to the spirit. And the three forces which were seen and felt to be actually producing these blessed effects were, the Church, the Bible, and the Prayer Book.

All this you must realize before you can understand the kind of enthusiasm, devoted attachment, and unlimited faith, which George Herbert, in common with the reformers, bishops, and clergy of the Church of England, professed for that admirable religious institution.

The Reformed Church, with its Reformed Prayer Book, and open Bible : armed with these, George Herbert seems to have felt he could go anywhere, and do anything. The most hardened sinner, the most open infidel, might easily be converted, if he could be enticed into the church, where he could not fail to be fascinated by its admirable services.

Indeed, I would to God we had this same spirit, which Keble has done much to revive in our day with his "Christian Year." I would that we could pour life once more into the formularies, so that they might reach the hearts of the people. And if we take George Herbert's hints we shall be able to do something towards this, for he worked from the spirit within to the letter without, and found fervour in the Prayer Book because he brought devotion in his heart. Yet was George Herbert the last man to be under bondage to forms; he understood their right function; "because they are the earthen vessel which contains the living treasure, therefore should they be made the fit receptacle of it."

Hear him, then, on the Prayer Book: his deep faith is calm and sober, and in it we indeed miss the high temperature, and religious passion of Keble; but on the other hand he is very direct and straightforward, and free alike from dryness and exaggeration.

THE BOOK OF COMMON PRAYER.

"What, prayer by the book? and common?
   Yes. Why not?
   The spirit of grace
   And supplication
    Is not left free alone
   For time and place;
But manner too. To read, or speak by rote,
   Is all alike to him that prays
   With 's heart that with his mouth he says
 They that in private by themselves alone
    Do pray, may take
   What liberty they please

> In choosing of the ways
>   Wherein to make
> Their souls' most intimate affections known
>   To Him that sees in secret, when
>   They are most conceal'd from other men.
>
> But he that unto others leads the way
>   In public prayer,
>   Should choose to do it so
>   As all that hear may know
>   They need not fear
> To tune their hearts unto his tongue, and say
>   Amen; nor doubt they were betray'd
>   To blaspheme when they should have pray'd.
>
> Devotion will add life unto the letter.
>   And why should not
>   That which authority
>   Prescribes esteemed be
>   Advantage got?
> If the prayer be good, the commoner the better.
>   Prayer in the church's words, as well
>   As sense, of all prayers bears the bell."

And when he comes to the pulpit he is still more homely; indeed I think we hear in the voice of George Herbert almost the last of our great Reformation preachers and humourists of the pulpit. The strange and forcible language of Ridley and Latimer was no doubt a great reaction from the wretched homilies and Latin discourses; and in truth, homeliness is a gift which the pulpit is constantly losing, and as constantly compelled to recover if souls are to be won. Indeed so parched up have congregations been with the dryness and formality of preaching, that some have openly declared that anything which is likely to do a man good, is good enough for the pulpit. You, my friends, who may sometimes criticize the fulness and freedom of pulpit speech, would be astonished were you to read some of the sermons of Ridley and Latimer: you would think them extremely coarse; and sometimes they were so flatly humorous that the people were quite unable to keep their countenances while those good men preached. We need not disguise the fact. Some of the greatest preachers have also been the great humorists. Indeed Carlyle, the saddest of living moralists and lay preachers, is also the greatest living humorist. It is also observable that the most noted Italian and French preachers of our own century have been habitually obliged to restrain the spontaneous ebullitions of feeling, which their forcible contrasts and living thrusts have called forth. And I can well believe that George Herbert was such an one, and that if he could sometimes bring home a truth by a vigorous simile and more vigorous contrast, he would not hesitate to make a man feel the absurdity of his behaviour, where he might have failed to convince him of its sin. Some men may be shamed into the performance of that which the moral sense alone is too feebly developed to enforce; so that when George Herbert treats of the pulpit in this poem, you will see how quaint he is, how unscrupulous in his use of surprises, and in the swift scene-shifting of speech:

> " 'Tis dinner-time; and now I look
> For a full meal. God send me a good cook;
> This is the dresser-board, and here
> I wait in expectation of good cheer.
> I'm sure the Master of the house
> Enough to entertain his guests allows;
> And not enough of some one sort alone,
> But choice of what best fitteth every one.
>
> God grant me taste and stomach good:
> My feeding will diversify my food.
> 'Tis a good appetite to eat,
> And good digestion, that makes good meat.
> The best food in itself will be,
> Not fed on well, poison, not food, to me.
> Let him that speaks look to his words; my ear
> Must careful be, both what and how I hear.

* * * * *

> Like an invited guest I will
> Be bold, but mannerly withal, sit still
>   And see what the Master of the feast
> Will carve unto me, and account that best
>   Which He doth choose for me, not I
> Myself desire; yea, though I should espy
> Some fault in the dressing, in the dishing, or
> The placing, yet I will not it abhor.
>
> So that the meat be wholesome, though
> The sauce shall not be toothsome, I'll not go
>   Empty away, and starve my soul,
> To feed my foolish fancy; but control
>   My appetite to dainty things,
> Which oft instead of strength diseases brings:
> But, if my pulpit-hopes shall all prove vain,
> I'll back into the reading pew again."

And in another place, on dull preaching: "Do not grudge to pick out treasures from an earthen pot. The worst speak something good: if all want sense, God takes a text and preaches patience."

Of pithy aphorisms there is indeed no end:

> "A verse may find him who a sermon flies."

Or on drinking too much,—

> "It is most just to throw that on the ground;
> Which would throw me there if I kept the round."

Or upon getting into debt,—

> "By no means run in debt; take thine own measure;
> Who cannot live on twenty pounds a year, cannot on forty."

Of course, you will remember that 20*l.* a year in those days was not what 20*l.* is now, but represented a much larger sum. Or on gambling,—

> "Play not for gain, but sport.
> Who plays for more than he can lose with pleasure
> Breaks his heart, perhaps his wife's too,
> And whom she bore."

The poem on money, called "Avarice," is a more sustained flight, but scarcely less pungent than these shorter utterances:

> "Money, thou bane of bliss, and source of woe,
> Whence comest thou, that thou art so fresh and fine?
> I know thy parentage is base and low:
> Man found thee, poor and dirty, in a mine.
>
> Surely thou didst so little contribute
> To this great kingdom which thou now hast got,
> That he was fain, when thou wast destitute,
> To dig thee out of thy dark cave and grot.
>
> Then forcing thee, by fire he made thee bright;
> Nay, thou hast got the face of man; for we
> Have with our stamp and seal transferr'd our right:
> Thou art the man, and man but dross to thee.
>
> Man calleth thee his wealth, who made thee rich;
> And while he digs out thee, falls in the ditch."

Now the "conceits" or, what we may call the affectations of George Herbert, belong to his period, and there are some very strange ones, with which we are not perhaps wholly in sympathy in these days; as for instance, when he writes a poem on the "Altar," and prints it in lines intended to represented the shape of an altar; or again, two verses called "Angels' Wings," printed in lines intended to represent wings. There are other verbal juggleries, which are not much in the taste of to-day, especially when applied to religious subjects; as where in a poem before alluded to he says that the name of Jesus is so dear to him, and that one day he broke the frame containing the letters of that sacred name, and was at first in despair to see all the letters J, E, S, U, fall on the ground. Then he picked them up and began to arrange them—first I, or J, then i, e, s, u, one after another in order, and was transported to find his new consolation in the discovery that, so treated, they made "I ease you"—Jesu!

There is another poem, which I will now cite, which abounds with what I must call the affectations of the age, showing the way in which literary men of Elizabeth's time played with their thoughts.

The poem is called "Paradise." It is constructed in this way; you take a word for the end of the first line, then the next line ends with the same word minus one letter, and the third line with the same word minus two letters, and so on. For instance, he begins with "grow" for the last word of the first line, and then follow "row," and "owe." Then come "start," "tart," and "art." Then the word "charm," which is followed by "harm" and "arm," and so on. Still this little poem, though hampered by this affected form, is so exquisite that unless attention were called to its quaint construction you would hardly notice it. Indeed "Paradise" is the perfection of poetic neatness:

> "I bless Thee, Lord, because I grow
> Among Thy trees, which in a row
> To Thee both fruit and order ow.
>
> What open force, or hidden charm,
> Can blast my fruit, or bring me harm
> While the enclosure is Thine arm?
>
> Inclose me still, for fear I start;
> Be to me rather sharp and tart,
> Than let me want thy hand and art.
>
> When thou dost greater judgments spare,
> And with thy knife but prune and pare,
> E'en fruitful trees more fruitful are.

> Such sharpness shows the sweetest friend:
> Such cuttings rather heal than rend:
> And such beginnings touch their end."

George Herbert's treatment of Death is peculiar. How different is the grim vision from Longfellow's Angel of Refuge bearing the tender blossom away to the fields of light above! very different too from Tennyson's veiled Nemesis, severing friend from friend; or from Keble's avenging Minister of Sin. George Herbert's Death is a sort of gaunt spectre, such as meets us in Holbein's "Dance of Death;" it is the once popular skull and cross-bones conception—grotesque, and somewhat ridiculous. Death occurs to George Herbert as a creature to be despised, to be flouted, to be trampled under foot, or to be held up to scorn. It is the voice of St. Paul, with a difference: "O Death, where is thy sting? O Grave, where is thy victory?" He looks into the grinning skull, and derides the miserable symbol of our perishable part, as if that could affront him with its vain terrors!

I notice that in the Elizabethan era—the age in which England was but half emancipated from Rome and its symbols—this was the prevailing tone of thought about Death. Not only was murder extremely popular on the stage, as might well be the case in an age accustomed to the wholesale massacre of religious persecution, and the public spectacle of torture; but the religious symbols of death, the accompaniments of Golgotha, were largely worn as ornaments, were treated and handled familiarly. Skulls were produced on the stage; ladies wore cross-bones in gold, and ivory, and silver; and the watches of gallants were made in the shape of skulls. Was it a semi-religious instinct, conserving at any cost the images which met the eye of the Catholic devotee on every altar, and at the foot of every crucifix? Or was it the wanton and irreverent treatment of objects which but lately had been associated with the highest religious rites—rites now repudiated as Popish, and mocked at in the fervour of the reformed faith? Perhaps both instincts mingled, and help to explain the fascination and wide popularity of the ignoble grotesque Death, together with the semi-ridicule apparent alike in Germany's great painter, Holbein, and in England's great poet, George Herbert. But how pungent and easily triumphant is the Christian's short dialogue with the skeleton!

"*Chr.* Alas, poor Death! where is thy glory?
Where is thy famous force, thy ancient sting?

Dea. Alas, poor mortal, void of story!
     Go spell and read how I have kill'd thy King.

Chr. Poor Death! and who was hurt thereby?
     Thy curse being laid on Him who makest thee accurst.

Dea. Let losers talk; yet, thou shalt die:
     These arms shall crush thee.

Chr.   Spare not; do thy worst.
     I shall be one day better than before:
     Thou so much worse, that thou shalt be no more."

More sweet and solemn, but not less characteristic, is the following:

" Death, thou wast once an uncouth hideous thing,
    Nothing but bones,
    The sad effect of sadder groans:
Thy mouth was open but thou couldst not sing.

    *   *   *   *   *

But since our Saviour's death did put some blood
    Into thy face,
    Thou art grown fair and full of grace,
Much in request, much sought for as a good.

For we do now behold thee gay and glad,
    As at dooms' day,
    When souls shall wear their new array,
And all thy bones with beauty shall be clad.

Therefore we can go die asleep, and trust
    Half that we have
    Unto an honest faithful grave—
Making our pillows either down or dust."

I said that George Herbert seldom kindled into anything like poetic passion or fervour, but his verse is sometimes radiant with a certain chastened lustre, all the more effective because so brief, so condensed.

Here the short bursts of verse come fresh from the penitent heart, like the broken sobs of a child, as in " Discipline :"

> " Throw away Thy rod,
> Throw away Thy wrath
>   O my God;
> Take the gentle path.
>
> For my heart's desire
> Unto Thine is bent :
>   I aspire
> To a full consent.
>
> Not a word or look
> I affect to own ;
>   But by book,
> And Thy book alone.
>
> Though I fail, I weep :
> Though I halt in pace,
>   Yet I creep
> To the throne of grace.
>
> Then let wrath remove ;
> Love will do the deed :
>   For with love
> Stony hearts will bleed.

> Love is swift of foot;
> Love's a man of war,
>   And can shoot,
> And can hit from far.
>
> Who can 'scape his bow?
> That which wrought on Thee,
>   Brought Thee low.
> Needs must work on me.
>
> Throw away Thy rod:
> Though man frailties hath,
>   Thou art God;
> Throw away Thy wrath."

We have another form of devotional passion in the low, subdued, and poetic melancholy, rising at the close into a burst of Divine joy, in the little poem called "Virtue:"

> "Sweet day, so cool, so calm, so bright;
> The bridal of the earth and sky:
> The dew shall weep thy fall to-night,
>   For thou must die.
>
> Sweet rose, whose hue angry and brave
> Bids the rash gazer wipe his eye,
> Thy root is ever in its grave,
>   And thou must die.
>
> Sweet spring, full of sweet days and roses,
> A box where sweets compacted lie,
> My music shows ye have your closes,
>   And all must die.

> Only a sweet and virtuous soul,
> Like season'd timber, never gives;
> But though the whole world turn to coal,
> Then chiefly lives."

We cannot more fitly close our meditations on George Herbert, than by listening to a poem on the highest level of emotion ever reached by Herbert. It is almost of the nature of ejaculatory prayer, and represents that central principle of spiritual life which ever proclaims the silent, un-uttered, and unutterable thoughts to be beyond all words; and the speaker feeling this, yet feeling also impelled to utterance, his prayer comes forth, short and broken, like the confession of the publican who went up into the temple to pray. Begun in words, it has to be completed in silence; the Spirit has to make intercession; all we can do is to offer up the longing, loving, trusting heart in prostrate adoration. Indeed it is, as George Herbert calls it, "A True Hymn:"

> "My joy, my life, my crown!
> My heart was meaning all the day
> Somewhat it fain would say:
> And still it runneth, muttering, up and down,
> With only this, 'My joy, my life, my crown!'

Yet slight not these few words;
   If truly said, they may take part
   Among the best in art.
The fineness which a hymn or psalm affords,
Is when the soul unto the lines accords.

He who craves all the mind,
   And all the soul, and strength, and time,
   If the words only rhyme
Justly complains, that somewhat is behind
To make his verse, or write a hymn in kind.

Whereas if the heart be moved,
   Although the verse be somewhat scant,
   God doth supply the want:
As when the heart says (sighing to be approved)
'O, could I love!' and stops; God writeth, 'Loved.'"

VIII.
Wordsworth.
DIVERSE POEMS.

VIII.

Wordsworth.

DIVERSE POEMS.

IT is difficult within a short compass to give anything but a brief bird's-eye view of a writer so diffuse and elaborate as Wordsworth. His popularity has steadily waxed, whilst that of contemporary poets who thought themselves far his superiors, has waned; and although often voted dull by many who purchase his works without reading them, his poems have been treasured by thousands who have read them, without always being able to buy them. Wordsworth has taken this strong hold of our age, because he is deeply representative of the inextinguishable spirituality of the nineteenth century. We may smile at a good deal which, to use his own words about another writer, "is neither interesting in itself, nor can lead to anything which is interesting,"—" Lines composed after reading the Newspaper," or "To the Spade of a Friend," or " To his own Portrait;" but there are other lines which have passed into the language, and have the true ring:

> " The light that never was on sea or land."
>
> " The child is father to the man."
>
> " A creature not too bright or good
> For human nature's daily food."
>
> " We murder, to dissect ! "

And perhaps few people are aware that Mr. Matthew Arnold's now celebrated " Stream of Tendency," is from Wordsworth.

For an elaborate analysis of Wordsworth's mind and its progress, I may refer the reader to such careful studies as Mr. Stopford Brookes's " Wordsworth," in " Theology in the English Poets." To these excellent essays I am indebted to-night for many fruitful and beautiful thoughts, and I have also been assisted in the selection of some passages. Our thoughts now may be ranged conveniently under four heads: Wordsworth's relation to Nature, to Man, and Politics, and to Universal Religion.

I. NATURE AND MAN.—Nature in her sublime

aspects inspired those immortal descriptions of scenery which have never been surpassed:

> "The immeasurable height
> Of woods decaying, never to be decay'd;
> The stationary blast of waterfalls;
> And in the narrow rent, at every turn
> Winds thwarting winds, bewilder'd and forlorn."

But the infinitely little was equally dear to him, and is recorded with the same care, and force, and beauty. Indeed nothing escaped him. The familiar robin, the daisy—loved of Chaucer, the green linnet, the skylark, and small celandine, the soft nest of the wren,—all is registered in that detailed photography of words. And sometimes he almost becomes a part of what he sees. Take this glimpse as of the quiet levels of the Thames in summer:

> "The calm
> And dead still water lay upon my mind,
> Even with a weight of pleasure; and the sky,
> Never before so beautiful, sank down
> Into my heart, and held me like a dream."

In such perfect gems as "The Daffodils" we have the same tendency to become one with outward nature which belongs to the first stage in the poetic growth:

"I wander'd lonely as a cloud
　That floats on high o'er vales and hills,
When all at once I saw a cloud,
　A host, of golden daffodils—
Beside the lake, beneath the trees,
Fluttering and dancing in the breeze.

Continuous as the stars that shine
　And twinkle on the Milky Way,
They stretch'd in never-ending line
　Along the margin of a bay;
Ten thousand saw I at a glance,
Tossing their heads in sprightly dance.

The waves beside them danced, but they
　Outdid the sparkling waves in glee:
A poet could not but be gay
　In such a jocund company.
I gazed, and gazed, but little thought
What wealth the show to me had brought.

For oft when on my couch I lie,
　In vacant or in pensive mood,
They flash upon that inward eye
　Which is the bliss of solitude,
And then my heart with pleasure fills,
And dances with the daffodils."

In the next stage we find, not the poet reflecting nature, but nature reflecting the poet. The inanimate has become alive; it has a soul that meets the poet's soul, and catches his moods:

> "The gentleness of heav'n is on the sea :
> Listen! the mighty being is awake,
> And doth, with his eternal motion, make
> A sound like thunder everlastingly."

This is redeemed from pantheism by hearing in all the very voice of God. The whole creation brings him—

> "Authentic tidings of invisible things;"

and with the poet-priest you stand—

> "Pious beyond the intention of your thought,
> Devout above the meaning of your will."

Yet how deaf does man at times become, to this divine ministry of nature! how easily and selfishly absorbed in pleasure and business! how insensible to the low sweet monitor! how blind to the supernatural beauty!

> "The world is too much with us; late and soon,
> Getting and spending, we lay waste our powers.
> Little we see in nature that is ours;
> We have given our hearts away, a sordid boon!"

That world, which he alternately dreads and courts, which at once draws and repels him, was soon to absorb Wordsworth's eager nature—the world of men and women. Man and Politics were to leave as indelible a mark upon his soul as the mountain solitudes, or the activities of ocean, forest, or Alpine cataract; the stir of college life fascinated him with its complex variety of human nature; then, too, the great men of antiquity, the scholars, and philosophers, and poets, of more modern times, gave him a deeper insight into the dignity of the human mind, and the subtleties of the human heart. He went back to London, forgetting for a time his mountain solitudes, and began to watch with intense interest—

> "The endless stream of men and many things,
> Quick dance of colours, of light, and form,
> Theatre and burial-place of passions."

But this interest in crowded centres was a mood which in Wordsworth never lasted long, and was constantly relieved by exquisite pauses "of poetic sensibility, of which the matchless "Sonnet on Westminster Bridge," is a fine specimen:

> "Earth has not anything to show more fair!
> Dull would he be of soul who could pass by
> A sight so touching in its majesty.
> This city now doth like a garment wear
> The beauty of the morning: silent, bare,
> Ships, towers, domes, theatres, and temples, lie
> Open unto the fields and to the sky,
> All bright and glittering in the smokeless air.

> Never did sun more beautifully steep
> In his first splendour valley, rock, or hill;
> Ne'er saw I, never felt, a calm so deep
> The river glideth at his own sweet will!
> Dear God! the very houses seem asleep:
> And all that mighty heart is lying still!"

At length, oppressed with the life of the noisy city, its heart-rending spectacles of poverty, its harsh and intolerable contrasts of squalor and wealth, its abrupt transitions from innocence to vice, Wordsworth fled to the country again, and there once more he revelled in—

> "The vision of the hills
> Those hallow'd and pure motions of the sense,
> That quiet independence of the heart,"

which came to him,

> "In the still spirit shed from evening air."

Here he gladly turned from the despondency bred in him by the contemplation of men in the crowded centres of life, to the pure and simple lives of little children. The famous "We are Seven," need hardly be quoted; to the same class belongs the following exquisite address "To a Young Girl:"

> "Dear child, dear girl, that walkest with me here,
> If thou appear untouch'd with solemn thought
> Thy nature is not therefore less divine;
> Though liest in Abraham's bosom all the year,
> And worship'st at the Temple's inner shrine,
> God being with thee when we know it not."

The poet sometimes forgot the popular theology of his day, which taught that every one was a child of sin, and that each one ought to have a consciousness of it. Many a theologian, perhaps not quite so close a student of nature as Wordsworth, has been scandalized by that simple address to one of his daughters, in which he alludes to her "sinless progress" through a world—

> "By sorrow darken'd and by care disturb'd;"

and then compares her to the moon,

> "Fair are ye both, and both are free from sin."

But the study of man is henceforth never to be wholly cast aside; the human drama, though too oppressive for prolonged contemplation in cities, is still a recurrent theme—the *mise en scène* only is shifted. Wordsworth becomes the poet of the poor, and on wayside hills in lonely hamlets, he pens, in lines of quiet force and truth, many annals of a quiet life. Now it is the shepherd and the last of the flock, or the forsaken beggar girl; the criminal swinging in chains; the poor bed-ridden old woman; the waggoner with his team; the idiot boy; the gipsies at their camp-fire. To this class belongs that example of perfect simplicity, brevity, and pathos, quite unequalled of its kind;

> "She dwelt among the untrodden ways
>   Beside the springs of Dove,
> A maid whom there were few to praise,
>   And very few to love;
> A violet by a mossy stone
>   Half hidden from the eye!
> Fair as a star, when only one
>   Is shining in the sky.
> She lived unknown, and few could know
>   When Lucy ceased to be;
> But she is in her grave, and oh!
>   The difference to me!

II. POLITICS.—But poet of the hill and hamlet as he was, it is impossible to separate Wordsworth from politics, or his politics from his poetry. As his religious and social views find their expression and development in those long, and, to many, wearisome works, the "Prelude" and the "Excursion," so do his political views find illustration chiefly in his shorter poems and sonnets.

The rise of the French Revolution was full of promise and hope. The brotherhood of man—the destruction of tyranny—the creation of an ideal society,—these were then the universal ideas "in the air."

No movement was ever more trusted by good men than the agitation begun under the clever, but questionable, auspices of such social reformers as Voltaire, Rousseau, and the Encyclopædists.

Wordsworth held on to the Revolution up to 1793, when he was staggered by the Reign of Terror, the excesses of Robespierre, and the murder of Louis XVI.

Still he was horrified at England's declaration of war, and steadily resisted the Napoleonic craze which followed, and from the entire dominion of which half a century has barely sufficed to set France and Europe free.

He calls it—

> "An accursed thing to gaze
> On prosperous tyrants with a dazzled eye;"

and lashes mercilessly the statesmen, who were as eager in 1802 to acknowledge the Divine right of Napoleon I., as were the statesmen in 1847 to accept Napoleon III.:

> "Lords, lawyers, statesmen,
>   Post forward all   *   *
>   *   *   to bend the knee
> In France before the new-born majesty.
> 'Tis ever thus. Ye men of prostrate mind,
> A seemly reverence may be paid to power;
> But truth and loyal virtue, never sown
> In haste, now springing with a transient shower,
> When truth, when sense, when liberty were flown."

And this is the appeal to England:

> "What hardship had it been to wait an hour?
>   Shame on you, feeble heads to slavery prone."

The doctrine of accomplished facts had not then become so entire a part of European politics, as the suppression of Poland, the unification of Germany and Italy, and the successful independence of America, have since made it.

The war-craze which, from time to time seizes hold of generations which have had no practical experience of its horrors, is firmly and consistently denounced, and the higher elements of national greatness indicated:

> "'Tis not in battles that from youth we train
>   The governors who must be wise and good."

The real greatness of a nation lies in the

observance of moral law, and the time-honoured precepts of the ancient prophets,—

> "Patience, temperance,
> Honour that knows the path and will not swerve,
> And piety towards God."

The true glory of man must ever spring from "plain living and high thinking."

But Wordsworth was at heart a thorough Englishman, and could rise on occasion into a fine, patriotic fervour, as, for example, in the sonnets on the battle of Waterloo, beginning—

> "Intrepid sons of Albion!"

The Revolution failed; and with that failure a sort of despair of the great world's commonwealth seemed to seize upon most of the better spirits. The reform of France was wrecked by the personal ambition of Napoleon; the excesses of the Revolution disgraced the name of liberty; the dream of a golden age ended in the Reign of Terror and the tyranny of Robespierre; and the guilty time only gave way to the despotism of an unscrupulous soldier, and a war policy which decimated France and drowned Europe in blood.

Still, undismayed by the French *fiasco*, Wordsworth remained to the end of his life the champion of oppressed nationalities. Switzerland, Spain, and Italy engaged his sympathies in turn ; and no one can read his series of sonnets, dedicated to national independence and liberty, without feeling that he was more than a patriot—a true citizen of the world, and an apostle of humanity.

But there was a political sense in which it may be said that Wordsworth never got over the disappointment of the French Revolution. As old age drew on, he retired more and more from the position of an advanced thinker, and grew strangely illiberal : so true was it that the French Revolution retarded for half a century the great cause of reform in this country—the correction of social abuses, and the ascendancy of representative government generally. Every beneficial change was at once denounced as revolution ; and the bloody days in Paris were for years pointed to by the timid fingers of political cowardice.

And Wordsworth shared this unwise and unworthy feeling. He opposed the Bill for admitting Nonconformists, as dangerous to monarchy and social order ; he advocated the removal of civil disabilities, but denounced Catholic emancipation ;

and in 1832 declared that the British Constitution would be destroyed by the Reform Bill.

He was sixty-two years old; he had lost his hopefulness: he had seen one revolution abroad, and he had not courage to face what he believed would end in another one at home. Still he retained, down to the last, a lively sympathy with Italy in her oppressed and pillaged condition, and prophesied for her an independence which we have only late in the nineteenth century seen realized.

But looking at Wordsworth's noblest work, nothing can dim the value of his contributions to the cause of universal religion. He had indeed lost his faith in the all-sufficiency of political theories to save society, but he had not lost his faith in human nature. In the darkest hour of the Revolution he could see, in the breakdown of old tyrannies, the overthrow of God's enemies; in the vilest depths of human depravity he found gleams of nobility and the protest of virtue—faithful unto death.

> "Thus moderated, thus composed, I found
> Once more in man an object of delight,
> Of pure imagination, and of love."

III. UNIVERSAL RELIGION.—The theology of Wordsworth—in so far as he had any—is neither better nor worse than the theology of his time. It was best when he forgot all about it. The ecclesiastical sonnets show all the sectarian bitterness of his age, and more than the bitterness of ours, against Roman Catholics, together with his admiration of Protestantism—a watchword so anxiously repudiated by an influential section of the Established Church of to-day, as equally disgraceful and historically inaccurate.

With these questions we are not now greatly concerned; but the real secret of the eager Wordsworth revival is to be sought for in neither his politics nor his theology. In an age of materialism, when specialities in science continue to score triumph after triumph, there seems to lie in Wordsworth's intense, masterful, and many-sided spirituality, a sort of irresistible fascination, as if the mind found in him the recovery of its lost balance, and escaped from matter—the thing which can be weighed and measured—to bathe itself in spirit—the thing which cannot be weighed and measured, and yet that which gives its only value and interest, some have said its very existence, to all that is weighed and measured. Demonstrate as you will—"murder to dissect"—you cannot convince the world for any length of time, or with permanent success, that we are but cunningly-devised mechanisms, irresponsible automata, and that, being such, our little life is "rounded by a sleep;" whilst others hope and *argue* that we are "spirits," and that there is an underlying, undying soul of all things in the universe which is self-conscious, and hath communion with man, Wordsworth the poet, the seer, *felt* it.

He felt it in the soul of nature like a "central peace subsisting at the heart of endless agitation." He felt it stirring in the depths of man's nature—

> "A pleasure, quiet and profound,
> Of permanent and universal sway,
> And permanent belief."

He felt it in the interlaced and interpenetrating influence of the great *Oversoul:*

> "That Being that is in the clouds and air,
> That is in the green leaves among the groves,
> Whose dwelling is the light of setting suns,
> And the round ocean and the evening air.
> Wisdom and Spirit of the Universe,
> Thou Soul that art the eternity of thought,
> And givest form to images, a breath,

> And everlasting motion; not in vain,
> By day or starlight, thus from my first dawn
> Of childhood, didst thou intertwine for me
> The passions which build up a human soul."

This is the Spirit that impels all thinking things, all objects of all thought, and rolls through all things.

It is in such strains that Wordsworth becomes the singer and teacher of our own restless, excited, and materialistic age; and taking up, in its enduring power and popularity, his "Ode on the Immortality of the Soul," we may well substitute for the "recollections of early childhood" the "discoveries of modern science," and exclaim, without in the least depreciating their immense importance and practical value—

> "Not for these I raise
> The song of thanks and praise;
> But for those obstinate questionings
> Of sense and outward things,
> Fallings from us, vanishings,
> Blank misgivings of a creature
> Moving about in worlds not realized,
> High instincts before which our mortal nature
> Did tremble like a guilty thing surprised;
> But for those first affections,
> Those shadowy recollections,
> Which, be they what they may,

Are yet the fountain-light of all our day,
Are yet a master-light of all our seeing;
Uphold us—cherish—and have power to make
Our noisy years seem moments in the being
Of the eternal silence: truths that wake
      To perish never:
Which neither listlessness, nor mad endeavour,
      Nor man, nor boy,
Nor all that is at enmity with joy,
Can utterly abolish or destroy!
  Hence, in a season of calm weather,
      Though inland far we be,
Our souls have sight of that immortal sea
    Which brought us hither;
    Can in a moment travel thither,
And see the children sport upon the shore,
And hear the mighty waters rolling evermore.

IX.
The Golden Treasury.
GLEANINGS.

IX.

The Golden Treasury.

GLEANINGS.

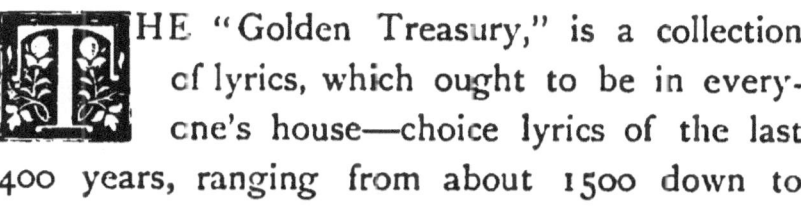HE "Golden Treasury," is a collection of lyrics, which ought to be in everyone's house—choice lyrics of the last 400 years, ranging from about 1500 down to 1850, but not including the works of any living poet. In my reference and treatment I am to-night limited by certain considerations. In the first place, I do not treat of anything in the pulpit which is not more or less of an "edifying" character; it must have something to point a moral, as well as to adorn a tale; it should rouse our aspirations, broaden our views, enrich our experiences of human life—or prompt hopeful and ennobling action; and of course a great deal of lyrical poetry in every age is not of this description.

Then the word "lyrical" limits us. "Lyric" means a short song, such as might be thrown off by a minstrel striking his lyre to some brief but passionate mood of thought and feeling: and the number of such short songs in the English language is limited. And then we are guided again by a certain standard of perfection. In the "Golden Treasury" only the most choice and beautiful specimens of each kind find a place. These requirements—that the poems should be lyrical, that they should be perfect, and that they should possess either directly or indirectly an edifying tendency—greatly restrict our field of choice. There is another consideration which applies to the present exposition, viz., that a great deal of the deeper spiritual poetry of the nineteenth century, in the "Golden Treasury," will not come under our notice at all in this lecture, because it is discussed in the other lectures; as, for instance, the moral and religious aspects of Tennyson, Longfellow, Keble, and Wordsworth; and remember, that in leaving out Wordsworth's name from the Golden Treasury, we leave out that of the most voluminous spiritual singer of the nineteenth century.

I. 1500–1600.—In following the order of this book, I gather from the first selection of poems, between 1500 and 1600, two, and but two, of Shakespeare's, and both very brief.

Now, there is a peculiarity about Shakespeare's poetry which I have dealt with elsewhere ("Shakespeare and the Stage"). He is full of verve, and spiritual sympathy with human nature, although his teaching does not lie peculiarly in a spiritual form, either in the way of doctrine or practice—least of all is he a dogmatist. His force lies in the fact that he takes deep and comprehensive views of human life, and feels how many-sided it is, and is resolved to leave no side of it uncanvassed, no depths unsounded; whether it be the force of sorrow, of disappointment, of joy, or hope, or despair, he deals with it thoroughly, he immerses himself in its element; and that is why after the study of Shakespeare, although no doctrine has been directly taught, no moral drawn, we rise up with a certain deepened sense of the value and mystery of life, and the possibilities of the soul. This is, indeed, not like pulpit teaching; would that pulpit teaching were more like it. But it is effective and spiritual teaching, because it dissipates the natural frivolity of the human mind, and leads us to feel how fearfully and wonderfully we are made. We are surprised into higher moods, we are filled with a sense of our own undeveloped capacities; we begin to move with larger strides, and breathe a more invigorating air.

The first fragment I lay before you, then, is a short poem called "Winter." In it Shakespeare seems to stand outside himself; and some of the most effective teaching in poetry or prose is where a man stands thus outside, and treats of himself as though he were somebody else. He thus passes in contemplative review different sides of his nature. In "Winter," Shakespeare takes a firm hold of those common experiences which come to us all sooner or later—the love of life, the sense of its transience, the mournful feeling of the gliding years, and how little use we have made of them,—and yet how we have loved them, how we weep for them, how hard it is to part from youth, and from health, and from pleasure—to lose sensibility, but not the longing for it—to feel our capacities for enjoyment stiffening, the avenues of the senses closing. It is the inexorable flow of the shining river of life, out of the darkness into the sunny world, and towards the dim ocean beyond. Ah!

how fain would we stay that swift, inexorable torrent; but we cannot; we can only stand on the brink of the rolling tide, and utter the natural plaint of the human spirit over life, clinging fondly to it, and more fondly, as it is passing so sadly and certainly away. Although these are not exactly religious views, yet they are sobering views, which indirectly suggest much that is profoundly moral and religious.

> "That time of year thou may'st in me behold
> When yellow leaves, or none, or few, do hang
> Upon those boughs which shake against the cold—
> Bare ruin'd choirs, where late the sweet birds sang.
>
> In me thou seest the twilight of such day
> As after sunset fadeth in the west,
> Which by and by black night doth take away,
> Death's second self, that seals up all in rest.
>
> In me thou seest the glowing of such fire
> That on the ashes of his youth doth lie
> As the deathbed whereon it must expire,
> Consumed with that which it was nourish'd by.
>
> This thou perceiv'st, which makes thy love more strong—
> To love that we'l which thou must leave ere long."

No great soul succumbs to final melancholy; and the hopefulness of Shakespeare is one of the chief elements of his enduring power, the buoyancy and saneness of the man which enables him, whilst bowing to the mystery of pain and loss, and thrilling to every sorrow, still to make the best of all human comfort, and get the most out of all human love. He rates at its highest value every gleam of friendship and affection. He is filled with ecstasy at the memory of joys which are not near him when he writes, but which soothe him out of the distance. Is there not a spirit, seizing upon and refreshing our spirit, in such an experience as comes forth glowing in the sweet poem which he calls "Consolation," where the man is extremely dejected, owing to a variety of causes, and suddenly remembers the glory which love sheds over life, and rises out of the winter of his discontent into the buoyancy of spring-time, remembering that although much has been taken away from him, there still remains one true heart in the world, and as long as there is one heart which beats in time with his, why should he despond?

What a lesson is this for many of us! You who have true friends—you who have living ones, who may not, perhaps, be near you now—what a glow should kindle up within you, when you think that

God strews your path with these, the flowers of affection! They will fade, no doubt, but they are not faded yet; you still have them here for your solace and dear remembrance:

> " When to the sessions of sweet silent thought
> I summon up remembrance of things past,
> I sigh the lack of many a thing I sought,
> And with old woes new wail my dear time's waste.
>
> Then can I drown an eye, unused to flow,
> For precious friends hid in death's dateless night,
> And weep afresh love's long-since-cancell'd woe,
> And moan the expense of many a vanish'd sight.
>
> Then can I grieve at grievances foregone,
> And heavily from woe to woe tell o'er
> The sad account of fore-bemoanéd moan,
> Which I new pay as if not paid before?
>
> But if, the while, I think on thee, dear friend,
> All losses are restored, and sorrows end."

II. 1600–1700.—You will not be surprised if, in passing from the fifteenth to the sixteenth century, I open first at Milton, and take from him the key-note of that great period.

Milton went up to college at the time of the accession of Charles I. He lived through all that critical period, witnessed the Protectorate of Oliver Cromwell, witnessed the Restoration, and he reflects in himself the close of one and the dawn of another great literary, social, and political epoch. He lived in the after-glow of Shakespeare's age; and although he might have seen Shakespeare in his very early youth, yet he escaped the affectations and conceits of the Elizabethan period, while retaining all its power and imagination. He was a Puritan of the Puritans, and yet no fanatic in his Puritanism. He was a Republican of the Republicans, and yet no lover of revolutions, and no bloodthirsty supporter of anarchy. He lived just before the period when the form of English poetry became stiff, accurate, and precise, but as cold as it was polished, in the works of Dryden and Pope. Milton caught a foretaste of that technical finish, without which no poetry is now acceptable as a work of art. But he never was soiled by a taint of the foul ribaldry and licentiousness which disgraced the poets of the Restoration.

He thus retained the finest human elements of the Elizabethan age, and united to them the art and refinement of an age the full development of which he did not live to see.

The distinguishing quality of Milton is his

breadth. Breadth is that indescribable impression produced in art by curves that form parts of very large circles; in music the same feeling is realized in listening to certain majestic phrases of Handel, Beethoven, and Wagner. Milton is solemn and grandiose, never dull, dreary, or pedantic; his poetry is always lit up, not only with an imaginative glow, but with an incomparable roll of glorious music, like the sound of the full organ in some cathedral aisle. If I read you a few lines expressive of the state of the world at the time of Christ's advent, when the great glory of the advent is represented as casting a morning radiance, like the rising sun, over the nations, how firm is the strain! how stately and rhythmical the cadences!

> "No war, or battle's sound,
> Was heard the world around:
> The idle spear and shield were high up hung;
> The hookéd chariot stood
> Unstain'd with hostile blood;
> The trumpet spake not to the arméd throng;
> And kings sat still, with awful eye,
> As if they surely knew their sovran Lord was by.
>
> But peaceful was the night
> Wherein the Prince of Light

> His reign of peace upon the earth began:
> The winds, with wonder whist,
> Smoothly the waters kist,
> Whispering new joys to the wild oceán—
> Who now hath quite forgot to rave,
> While birds of calm sit brooding on the charméd wave."

It may seem unnatural even to speak of Milton apart from the "Paradise Lost," but all fragments from that great work are excluded to-night because I am referring only to poems contained in a book of songs and lyrics. Yet does the "Paradise Lost" sound the key-note of his genius.

Milton was emphatically a religious poet. There breathes throughout his work an undertone of deep piety, which assumes a touching and personal solemnity when it comes to be associated with the great affliction of his life. He who so well described "flowers of all hue" and "trembling leaves," the "orient sun" and "the five wandering fires," was himself blind!

In the "Samson Agonistes" we have a wonderful and sympathetic record of his own state—the blind physical hero speaks for the blind intellectual giant; and another giant of emotional expression, Handel, has set to music the thoughts of his brother in the sister art.

But as drama we must exclude the famous passage beginning:

> "O dark, dark, dark amid the blaze of noon,
> Irrevocably dark—total eclipse."

I select another passage, of more quiet and devotional beauty, if not of more enduring power:

> "When I consider how my light is spent
> Ere half my days, in this dark world and wide,
> And that one talent which is death to hide
> Lodged with me useless, though my soul more bent
>
> To serve therewith my Maker, and present
> My true account, lest He, returning, chide—
> Doth God exact day-labour, light denied?
> I fondly ask. But Patience, to prevent
>
> That murmur, soon replies : God doth not need
> Either man's work, or His own gifts: who best
> Bear His mild yoke, they serve Him best. His state
> Is kingly; thousands at His bidding speed,
> And post o'er land and ocean without rest:—
> They also serve who only stand and wait."

In these days of technical finish our smallest poets are expected to achieve a polish not always reached in Elizabethan times by the greatest masters. Yet it would be hard to find in poetry, ancient or modern, a higher grace and finish,

T

combined with extreme sweetness and simplicity, than in Milton's "Lycidas." The note of elegiac pain is first sounded, then comes the plaintive narration, which is rounded off and played upon by the tender brooding of the mind, until it rises out of its own melancholy into a semi-mythic, semi-religious triumph. Lycidas is a poem in memory of a friend drowned in the Irish Channel, and it takes the classical form congenial to the age when it is put into the mouth of a shepherd amenting the loss of his friend. I take a portion of it:

> "Yet once more, O ye laurels, and once more
> Ye myrtles brown, with ivy never sere,
> I come to pluck your berries harsh and crude,
> And with forced fingers rude
> Shatter your leaves before the mellowing year.
> Bitter constraint, and sad occasion dear
> Compels me to disturb your season due:
> For Lycidas is dead, dead ere his prime,
> Young Lycidas, and hath not left his peer:
> Who would not sing for Lycidas? He knew
> Himself to sing, and build the lofty rhyme.
> He must not float upon his watery bier
> Unwept, and welter to the parching wind
> Without the meed of some melodious tear."

Then follows the mourning for Lycidas by

various voices of nature personified; and finally the closing note of hope and consolation is struck: the memories of the sweet friend must not close in sorrow.

"'Weep no more, woeful shepherds, weep no more;
For Lycidas, your sorrow, is not dead,
Sunk though he be beneath the watery floor:
So sinks the day-star in the ocean-bed,
And yet anon repairs his drooping head,
And tricks his beams, and with new-spangled ore
Flames in the forehead of the morning sky.
So Lycidas sank low, but mounted high
Through the dear might of Him that walk'd the waves,
Where, other groves and other streams along,
With nectar pure his oozy locks he laves,
And bears the unexpressive nuptial song
To the blest kingdoms meek of joy and love.
There entertain him all the saints above
In solemn troops, and sweet societies,
That sing, and singing, in their glory move,
And wipe the tears for ever from his eyes.
Now, Lycidas the shepherds weep no more;
Henceforth thou art the Genius of the shore
In thy large recompense, and shalt be good
To all that wander in that perilous flood.'

Thus sang the uncouth swain to the oaks and rills,
While the still morn went out with sandals gray;
He touch'd the tender stops of various quills,
With eager thought warbling his Doric lay:

> And now the sun had stretch'd out all the hills,
> And now was dropt into the western bay:
> At last he rose, and twitch'd his mantle blue:
> To-morrow to fresh woods, and pastures new."

"Lycidas" is also remarkable for the number of lines which, in so short a poem, have worked themselves into our common stock of phrases and quotations. "The hungry sheep look up, and are not fed"—which is so commonly applied to poor, thin preaching. People assemble devoutly hungry, desiring nothing so much as to imbibe something good and nourishing; they look up to the shepherd, who gives them little or nothing to eat after all. You may have had this experience: the sermon was most unfortunate, it did you no good; "the hungry sheep look up, and are not fed." And yet it may not have been altogether the shepherd's fault. There is something in the hearer; and what has done you no good may have done good to some one else; still Milton's text is a useful one for the preacher, at all events, to engrave upon his heart. And no wonder that such lines as these have become familiar as they are immortal:—The day-star—

> "Flames in the forehead of the morning sky;"

the solemn troops—

> "That sing, and singing, in their glory move;"

and—

> "While the still morn went out with sandals gray;"

and the much-quoted and misquoted line (for "fields" is constantly substituted for "woods")—

> "To-morrow to fresh woods and pastures new;"

and lastly,—

> "That two-handed engine at the door
> Stands ready to smite once, but smite no more."

I take but one more poem from that century, and, strange to say, it is one of Herrick's, a man who wrote a great deal of frivolous poetry, but who was touched, for all that, with the true spirit of poetry, and in this sweet little song " To Daffodils" has shown how a man whose head was, alas! too often steeped in the fumes of wine, and who entered freely into the licentious enjoyments of that licentious age, was still capable of pure, fresh feelings, when he talks of beautiful things in nature which soothe the heart, and sometimes win the senses from gross or selfish indulgences. A little poem like the "Daffodils" falls upon the earth-worn spirit like spring rain upon the parched and dusty ground; Wordsworth is not more pure.

> "Fair Daffodils, we weep to see
>   You haste away so soon:
> As yet the early rising sun
>   Has not attain'd his noon.
>   Stay, stay,
>   Until the hasting day
>   Has run
>   But to the even-song;
> And, having pray'd together, we
>   Will go with you along.
>
> We have short time to stay as you;
>   We have as short a spring;
> As quick a growth to meet decay
>   As you, or any thing.
>   We die
>   As your hours do, and dry
>   Away,
>   Like to the Summer's rain;
> Or, as the pearls of morning's dew,—
>   Ne'er to be found again."

III. 1700–1800.—When we pass into the century 1700 to 1800, we come to the age of very great poetical finish, but very little poetical power. Still there were poets who produced some exquisite lines, and Gray was one of these. He wrote very little, but he never wrote anything that was not supremely excellent of its kind; and that kind of correctly-balanced, calm, and yet elegiac excellence, culminates in a poem which is familiar to every one, and which begins,—

"The curfew tolls the knell of parting day."

I need hardly quote it, but it certainly is noteworthy how each line of this poem possesses remarkable excellence individually, and doubtless that is why it is so popular. There is always good reason for a popularity which lasts, and that of Gray's "Elegy" is of the most enduring kind. We should perhaps love it better, if we had not had to learn it at school. The number of its lines which have passed into the language, the beauty of those lines, their singular capacity for wear and tear, without being worn out or torn to tatters, stamp them as of the first quality of thought and expression.

"Each in his narrow cell for ever laid,
The rude forefathers of the hamlet sleep."

We seldom pass a churchyard, and read the rude or quaint inscriptions of the village mason, without these lines rising in our memory, if not to our lips. Or—

> "Let not Ambition mock their useful toil,
> Their homely joys, and destiny obscure;
> Nor Grandeur hear with a disdainful smile
> The short and simple annals of the poor."

Or—

> "Can storied urn or animated bust
> Back to its mansion call the fleeting breath?
> Can Honour's voice provoke the silent dust,
> Or Flattery soothe the dull, cold ear of Death?"

How often, when recognizing singular merit in obscure places, have we thought of—

> "Some village Hampden, that with dauntless breast
> The little tyrant of his fields withstood,
> Some mute, inglorious Milton, here may rest,
> Some Cromwell, guiltless of his country's blood."

I have only time to revive the accustomed ring of such other lines as—

> "Far from the madding crowd's ignoble strife."
>
> "They kept the noiseless tenour of their way."
>
> "Nor cast one longing, lingering look behind."
>
> "E'en in our ashes live their wonted fires."

I may quote entire the shorter epitaph which stands at the close of the "Elegy:"

> "Here rests his head upon the lap of Earth,
> A Youth, to Fortune and to Fame unknown;

Fair Science frown'd not on his humble birth,
And Melancholy mark'd him for her own.

Large was his bounty, and his soul sincere;
Heaven did a recompense as largely send:
He gave to misery all he had, a tear,
He gain'd from heaven, 'twas all he wish'd, a friend.

No farther seek his merits to disclose,
Or draw his frailties from their dread abode
(There they alike in trembling hope repose),
The bosom of his Father and his God."

I close this period, which is stamped with a love of elegy, with two poems—first one of the saddest and sweetest songs of parting, by Lady Nairn:

"I'm wearing awa', Jean,
Like snaw when it's thaw, Jean,
I'm wearing awa'
    To the land o' the leal.

There's nae sorrow there, Jean,
There's neither cauld nor care, Jean;
The day is aye fair
    In the land o' the leal.

Ye were aye leal and true, Jean;
Your task's ended noo, Jean,
And I'll welcome you
    To the land o' the leal.

Our bonnie bairn's there, Jean,
She was baith guid and fair, Jean

> O, we grudged her right sair
>   To the land o' the leal!
>
> Then dry that tearfu' e'e, Jean,
> My soul langs to be free, Jean,
> And angels wait on me
>   To the land o' the leal.
>
> Now fare ye weel, my ain Jean;
> This warld's care is vain, Jean;
> We'll meet and aye be fain
>   In the land o' the leal."

And then a poem by Anna Lætitia Barbauld, perhaps the gentlest, soberest poem on death ever written, with just a quaint touch of George Herbert about it:

> "Life! I know not what thou art,
> But know that thou and I must part;
> And when, or how, or where, we met,
> I own to me's a secret yet.
>
> Life! we've been long together,
> Through pleasant and through cloudy weather;
> 'Tis hard to part when friends are dear—
> Perhaps 'twill cost a sigh, a tear;
>
> Then steal away; give little warning;
>   Choose thine own time;
> Say not Good Night,—but in some brighter clime
>   Bid me Good Morning."

IV. 1800–1850.—Passing to the last series of

poems, between 1800 and 1850, we seem to come to quite a different atmosphere—into the mid current of the nineteenth century. There is something of the feverish haste and restlessness about the poems which are characteristic of our age. The steady old business ways, occupations, manners— even the steady old dissipations, are all broken up; a change has come in with the new modes of locomotion, the new activity of the press, the new and prodigious developments of commerce and industry. The iron tyranny of Napoleon treads close on the bloody heels of the Revolution; and the ferment of Romanticism following the downfall of that tyranny, created an atmosphere of thought in which all genius fructified vigorously. Men began to live at high pressure—thought, talked, and worked faster, as though conscious that the springs of life might be quickly dried up in the fierce heat surrounding them, and that there were only a few hours of daylight left. The poet, the scholar, is oppressed with the thought that he may die without completing his life work. This is the case with Keats, who owned quite a first-class poetic faculty, yet never lived to develope his gift. He was fully conscious of this himself. In the "Terror of Death" we notice a feeling of uneasy haste—that horror of going down to the grave with his work undone, which has oppressed many a noble soul. Alas! in him it was prophetic, for it was true; he never lived to complete his work:

> "When I have fears that I may cease to be
> Before my pen has glean'd my teeming brain—
> Before high-piled books, in charact'ry,
> Hold like rich garners the full-ripen'd grain;
>
> When I behold, upon the night's starr'd face,
> Huge cloudy symbols of a high romance,
> And think that I may never live to trace
> Their shadows, with the magic hand of chance;
>
> And when I feel, fair Creature of an hour!
> That I shall never look upon thee more,
> Never have relish in the fairy power
> Of unreflecting love—then on the shore
>
> Of the wide world I stand alone, and think
> Till Love and Fame to nothingness do sink."

Charles Lamb gives us another phase of this nineteenth century feeling—its morbid introspection, its intense, recluse-like sensitiveness in the midst of crowds; the settled melancholy of him who sees his friends one by one drop off, and his path grow lonely as he himself nears the grave.

Yet all here is characteristic of the bustle and hurry of a life teeming with human interests, faces, occupations, from which in this stimulating age few can escape; all is spoken in the midst of a crowd. Lamb's is not exactly the verse of a regular poet; it is not rhyme, but a sort of rhythmic prose, bearing no mark of the file, yet finished in form, with a certain flow and integrity of deep feeling—as though the man's under-current of emotion had been too intense to range itself into regular periods of rhyme, but flowed out with a kind of suppressed and temperate sadness, which is inexpressibly touching :

"THE OLD FAMILIAR FACES.

I have had playmates, I have had companions
In my days of childhood, in my joyful school-days—
All, all are gone, the old familiar faces.

I have been laughing, I have been carousing,
Drinking late, sitting late, with my bosom cronies—
All, all are gone, the old familiar faces.

I loved a Love once, fairest among women :
Closed are her doors on me, I must not see her—
All, all are gone, the old familiar faces.

I have a friend, a kinder friend has no man :
Like an ingrate, I left my friend abruptly—
Left him, to muse on the old familiar faces.

> Ghost-like I paced round the haunts of my childhood;
> Earth seem'd a desert I was bound to traverse—
> Seeking to find the old familiar faces.
>
> Friend of my bosom, thou more than a brother,
> Why wert not thou born in my father's dwelling—
> So might we talk of the old familiar faces?
>
> How some they have died, and some they have left me,
> And some are taken from me; all are departed—
> All, all are gone, the old familiar faces."

I cannot close without giving you something from Shelley—that soul of flame, and wind, and perfume, which seems to resume in itself the wildest yet finest elements of the nineteenth century—restlessness, passion, and poetic insight. He has been often the butt of religious scorn and censure; and indeed, he revolted from the conventional views of religion which were offered him as the substance of things hoped for, as well as the evidence of things not seen. He fled thence to bathe himself in a wild natural religion of nature, which to his spirit may no doubt have become somewhat vague and pantheistic. He believed not in the God whom he found worshipped, or at all events preached, in churches and chapels; not because he would not fain have worshipped a God, but because his glowing and sensitive spirit recoiled from the contradictory and grotesque Deity of the popular theology whilst the narrow subjective ethics of Wesley held sway over the personal religion of the land. Such ancient vintages had lost their flavour for Percy Bysshe Shelley, too prophetic of the new thoughts and impulses of our century, only the first score years of which he was destined to see. The shepherds could not feed him; he fled alone into the wilderness, and found communion with woods, and fountains, and song-birds, and all the wild beauties of sea, vale, and mountain, in sunnier climes than ours. His soul seemed to take each influence, and become one with it in turn—now living and exulting in the wild crash of the tempest, and now bathed in the stillness of the summer noon. The earth, and sky, and sea, yielded up their secrets to Shelley, and he gave them multitudinous voices, and their voices are still ringing in our ears—we love them. He touched the threshold of a period he was not permitted to enter. Were he alive now we should take to our heart of hearts that flashing soul—that sweet wild bird, so full of passion and ecstasy—" cor cordium."

A close mystic sympathy with the Divine soul

in nature has never been so intensely realized and rendered as in some of those great bursts of poetic eloquence in which Shelley pours out his soul in a kind of child-like adoration of the outward and visible universe:

> " O wild West wind, thou breath of Autumn's being,
> Thou from whose unseen presence the leaves dead
> Are driven, like ghosts from an enchanter fleeing,
> Yellow, and black, and pale, and hectic red,
> Pestilence stricken multitudes: O, thou,
> Who chariotest to their dark wintry bed
> The winged seeds, where they lie cold and low,
> Each like a corpse within its grave, until
> Thine azure sister of the Spring shall blow
> Her clarion o'er the dreaming earth, and fill
> (Driving sweet buds like flocks to feed in air)
> With living hues and odours plain and hill:
> Wild spirit, which art moving everywhere;
> Destroyer and preserver; hear, O, hear!
> * * * * *
> If I were a dead leaf thou mightest bear;
> If I were a swift cloud to fly with thee—
> A wave to pant beneath thy power, and share
> The impulse of thy strength, only less free
> Than thou, O, uncontrollable! if even
> I were as in my boyhood, and could be
> The comrade of thy wanderings over heaven,
> As then, when to outstrip thy skiey speed
> Scarce seem'd a vision; I would ne'er have striven
> As thus with thee in prayer in my sore need.

Oh! lift me as a wave, a leaf, a cloud!
I fall upon the thorns of life! I bleed!
A heavy weight of hours has chain'd and bow'd
One too like thee: tameless, and swift, and proud.
Make me thy lyre, even as the forest is:
What if my leaves are falling like its own!
The tumult of thy mighty harmonies
Will take from both a deep, autumnal tone,
Sweet thought in sadness. Be thou, spirit fierce,
My spirit! Be thou me, impetuous one!
Drive my dead thoughts over the universe,
Like wither'd leaves to quicken a new birth!
Scatter, as from an unextinguish'd hearth
Ashes and sparks, my words among mankind!
Be through my lips to unawaken'd earth
The trumpet of a prophecy! O wind,
If winter comes, can spring be far behind?"

I close our meditations to-night with one sober little poem, which is a sweet and natural description of human life, which ordains that the years of childhood should seem long, long years, and that the years of middle life and old age shall speed rapidly away, like the swiftly falling sands in the inexorable hour-glass of time. It is an experience which most of us have had. We remember as children the long periods up to Christmas time, and the long drawn out summer months: how short they are now to some of us, now that the leaves of life are reddening, and the days draw in, and the shadows fall quickly! This little poem by Campbell is a perfect contrast to Shelley; it is sober, didactic, yet with a certain lightness of touch, and a tinge of pathos and regret, which saves it from the commonplace of Pope, or the dulness of Addison.

> " The more we live, more brief appear
>   Our life's succeeding stages:
> A day to childhood seems a year,
>   And years like passing ages.
>
> The gladsome current of our youth,
>   Ere passion yet disorders,
> Steals lingering like a river smooth
>   Along its grassy borders.
>
> But as the careworn cheek grows wan,
>   And sorrow's shafts fly thicker,
> Ye stars that measure life to man,
>   Why seem your courses quicker?
>
> When joys have lost their bloom and breath,
>   And life itself is vapid,
> Why as we reach the Falls of Death,
>   Feel we its tide more rapid?
>
> It may be strange—yet who would change
>   Time's course to slower speeding,
> When one by one our friends have gone,
>   And left our bosoms bleeding?

Heaven gives our years of fading strength
    Indemnifying fleetness;
And those of youth, a seeming length
    Proportion'd to their sweetness."

LONDON:
PRINTED BY GILBERT AND RIVINGTON, LD.,
ST. JOHN'S HOUSE, CLERKENWELL ROAD, E.C.

www.ingramcontent.com/pod-product-compliance
Lightning Source LLC
Chambersburg PA
CBHW032043230426
43672CB00009B/1453